Words That Wound

New Perspectives on Law, Culture, and Society

Robert W. Gordon and Margaret Jane Radin,
Series Editors

Words That Wound

Critical Race Theory, Assaultive Speech, and the First Amendment

Mari J. Matsuda, Charles R. Lawrence III,
Richard Delgado, and
Kimberlè Williams Crenshaw

Westview Press
BOULDER • SAN FRANCISCO • OXFORD

New Perspectives on Law, Culture, and Society

Copyright © 1993 by Mari J. Matsuda, Charles R. Lawrence III, Richard Delgado, and Kimberlè Williams Crenshaw

Chapter 2 reprinted with permission from Mari J. Matsuda, *Public Response to Racist Speech: Considering the Victim's Story,* 87 Mich. L. Rev. (August 1989); Chapter 3 reprinted with permission from Charles R. Lawrence III, *If He Hollers Let Him Go: Regulating Racist Speech on Campus,* Duke L.J. 431 (1990); Chapter 4 reprinted with permission from Richard Delgado, *Words That Wound: A Tort Action for Racial Insults, Epithets, and Name Calling,* 17 Harv. C.R.-C.L. L. Rev. 133 (1982)

Poetry excerpt on page 24 reprinted with permission from Lorna Dee Cervantes, *Emplumada,* (Pittsburgh: University of Pittsburgh Press). © 1981 by Lorna Dee Cervantes

Published in 1993 in the United States of America by Westview Press, Inc., 5500 Central Avenue, Boulder, Colorado 80301-2877, and in the United Kingdom by Westview Press, 36 Lonsdale Road, Summertown, Oxford OX2 7EW

Library of Congress Cataloging-in-Publication Data
Words that wound : critical race theory, assaultive speech, and the
    First Amendment / Mari J. Matsuda . . . [et al.].
    p.   cm. — (New perspectives on law, culture, and society)
    Includes bibliographical references and index.
    ISBN 0-8133-8427-3 (cloth). — ISBN 0-8133-8428-1 (pbk.)
    1. Libel and slander—United States.   2. Hate crimes—United
States.   3. Freedom of speech—United States.   4. Racism in
language.   I. Matsuda, Mari J., 1956–   II. Series.
KF9345.W67   1993
346.7303'4—dc20
[347.30634]   92-41562
                                                                                        CIP

Printed and bound in the United States of America

The paper used in this publication meets the requirements of the American National Standard for Permanence of Paper for Printed Library Materials Z39.48-1984.

10   9   8   7   6   5   4   3   2

Contents

1

Introduction

Charles R. Lawrence III, Mari J. Matsuda,
Richard Delgado, and Kimberlè Williams Crenshaw

This is a book about assaultive speech, about words that are used as weapons to ambush, terrorize, wound, humiliate, and degrade. Of late, there has been an alarming rise in the incidence of assaultive speech. Although this is hardly a new phenomenon—hate speech is arguably as American as apple pie—it is a social practice that has gained a new strength in recent years. Incidents of hate speech and racial harassment are reported with increasing frequency and regularity, particularly on American college campuses, where they have reached near epidemic proportions. The National Institute Against Prejudice and Violence in its 1990 report on campus ethnoviolence found that 65 to 70 percent of the nation's minority students reported some form of ethnoviolent harassment, and the number of college students victimized by ethnoviolence is in the range of 800,000 to 1 million annually.[1]

In response to this outbreak of hate speech, many universities and other public institutions have enacted regulations prohibiting speech that victimizes racial minorities and other historically subordinated groups. These regulations have prompted a heated and wide-ranging public debate over the efficacy of such regulations. Many believe that hate speech regulations constitute a grave danger to first amendment liberties, whereas others argue that such regulations are necessary to protect the rights of those who have been and continue to be denied access to the full benefits of citizenship in the United States. This debate has deeply divided the liberal civil rights/civil liberties community and produced strained relations within the membership of organizations like the American Civil Liberties Union (ACLU).

Those civil libertarians who favor restrictions on hate speech find themselves in a distinct minority. They are called "first amendment revisionists" and "thought police." It is not a coincidence that the strongest sentiment for regulating hate speech has come from members of victimized communities. Persons of color, women, gays, and lesbians are disproportionately

1

represented among those who support the sanctioning of hate speech, and the Jewish community is sharply divided on this issue.

This book is a collection of essays written by four of the leading advocates of public regulation of racially abusive hate speech. We do not attempt to present all sides of this debate. Rather we present a dissenting view grounded in our experiences as people of color and ask how those experiences lead to different understandings of racism and law. Our purpose here is to analyze a pressing public issue from within the emergent intellectual movement called critical race theory. In so doing we hope to provide our readers with insights that will be helpful to them as individuals, policymakers, and students of theory.

How has this book come to pass? What is the common ground that unites the work of the four authors? Are there generic themes, shared stories? Is there an ideology that makes our disparate work a whole? How and why is our work different from that of our white colleagues on the left or of those who describe themselves as liberals? What distinguishes our position from that of politicians and theorists on the right who have called for restrictions on speech?

The answers to these questions begin with our identities. We are two African Americans, a Chicano, and an Asian American. We are two women and two men. We are outsider law teachers who work at the margins of institutions dominated by white men. The identity that defines us, that brings our work together and sets it apart from that of most of our colleagues, is more complex than the categories of race and gender imposed upon us by a world that is racist and patriarchal. It is an identity shaped by life experience: by what parents and neighbors taught us as children; by our early encounters with the more blatant forms of segregation and racial exclusion and the contemporary confrontations with less obvious forms of institutional and culturally ingrained racism and sexism that face us each day; by our participation in the civil rights struggles of the 1960s and 1970s; and by the histories of the communities from which we come.

Our identities are also defined by choice. Each of us has chosen to identify with a tradition of radical teaching among subordinated Americans of color. The historian Vincent Harding describes this tradition as a vocation of struggle against dehumanization, a practice of raising questions about the reasons for oppression, an inheritance of passion and hope.[2] We inherited this tradition from parents and grandparents and from countless others who have resisted racial oppression, but Harding's description begins with the word "vocation." The inference is that one must *choose* to accept the gift and the burden of this inheritance. One must choose to embrace the values of humanism. One must choose to engage in the practice of liberationist teaching. One must make that choice each day. It is this voluntary association with the struggle that is the most important part of our common identity.

What Is Critical Race Theory?

Teachers of color in the legal academy who choose to join this tradition of radical teaching have sought, in their teaching and scholarship, to articulate the values and modes of analysis that inform their vocation of struggle. These efforts have produced an emerging genre known as critical race theory. Critical race theory is grounded in the particulars of a social reality that is defined by our experiences and the collective historical experience of our communities of origin. Critical race theorists embrace subjectivity of perspective and are avowedly political. Our work is both pragmatic and utopian, as we seek to respond to the immediate needs of the subordinated and oppressed even as we imagine a different world and offer different values. It is work that involves both action and reflection. It is informed by active struggle and in turn informs that struggle.

Critical race theory cannot be understood as an abstract set of ideas or principles. Among its basic theoretical themes is that of privileging contextual and historical descriptions over transhistorical or purely abstract ones. It is therefore important to understand the origins of this genre in relation to the particulars of history. Critical race theory developed gradually. There is no identifiable date of birth, but its conception can probably be located in the late 1970s. The civil rights movement of the 1960s had stalled, and many of its gains were being rolled back. It became apparent to many who were active in the civil rights movement that dominant conceptions of race, racism, and equality were increasingly incapable of providing any meaningful quantum of racial justice. Individual law teachers and students committed to racial justice began to meet, to talk, to write, and to engage in political action in an effort to confront and oppose dominant societal and institutional forces that maintained the structures of racism while professing the goal of dismantling racial discrimination.

The consciousness of critical race theory as a movement or group and the movement's intellectual agenda were forged in oppositional reaction to visions of race, racism, and law dominant in this post–civil rights period. At the same time, both the movement and the theory reflected assertions of a commonality of values and community that were inherited from generations of radical teachers before us.

Group identity forms in a way similar to individual identity. Its potential exists long before consciousness catches up with it. It is often only upon backward reflection that some kind of beginning is acknowledged. The same holds true of intellectual influences. Some influences are so significant that they become transparent, they fade into what becomes the dominant picture. Often it is not until one engages in a conscious reconstruction, asking what led to what else, that a history is revealed or, perhaps more accurately, chosen.

Kimberlè Crenshaw places the social origins of what was to become critical race theory at a student boycott and alternative course organized in 1981 at the Harvard Law School. The primary objective of the protest was to persuade the administration to increase the number of tenured professors of color on the faculty. The departure of Derrick Bell, Harvard's first African-American professor, to assume the deanship of the law school at the University of Oregon had left Harvard Law School with only two professors of color. Students demanded that the law school begin the rectification of this situation by hiring a person of color to teach "Race Racism and American Law," a course that had been regularly taught by Bell, who was also the author of a ground-breaking text on the subject. When it became apparent that the administration was not prepared to meet their demand, students organized an alternative course. Leading academics and practitioners of color were invited each week to lecture and lead discussion on a chapter from Bell's book.

This course served as one of several catalysts for the development of critical race theory as a genre and movement. It brought together in a common enterprise many of the legal scholars who were beginning to teach and write about race with activist students who were soon to enter the ranks of teaching. Kimberlè Crenshaw, then a student at Harvard, was one of the primary organizers of the alternative course. Mari Matsuda, a graduate student at the law school, was also a participant in the course. Richard Delgado and Charles Lawrence were among the teachers invited to give guest lectures. The course provided a forum for the beginnings of a collectively built discourse aimed at developing a full account of the legal construction of race and racism in this country.

The Harvard course was not the only place where teachers and students gathered to engage in this new enterprise. There were conferences, seminars, and study groups at law schools across the nation. A small but growing group of scholars committed to finding new ways to think about and act in pursuit of racial justice began exchanging drafts of articles and course materials. We gave each other support and counsel by phone, as each of us struggled in isolation in our own institutions. We met in hotel rooms before, during, and after larger law school conferences and conventions. Slowly a group identity began to take shape.

Some of us sought intellectual community in what was then the dominant progressive movement in the law schools, critical legal studies. Critical legal studies, originating among a predominantly white group of law professors identified with the left, had attracted a small but significant group of scholars of color who were, to varying degrees, alienated from dominant liberal approaches to the law and legal education and were looking for both progressive allies and a radical critique of the law. Many of these colleagues on the white left had worked with us during the civil rights and antiwar movements of the 1960s and some of them continued to be important sources of support to our efforts to integrate law school student bodies and faculties and make law school curricula and legal scholarship more responsive to the needs of subordinated communities of color.

Even within this enclave on the left we sometimes experienced alienation, marginalization, and inattention to the agendas and a misunderstanding of the issues we considered central to the work of combating racism. Scholars of color within the left began to ask their white colleagues to examine their own racism and to develop oppositional critiques not just to dominant conceptions of race and racism but to the treatment of race within the left as well.

By the mid-1980s this motley band of progressive legal scholars of color had produced a small but significant body of scholarship, and a sense of group identity began to emerge. This group identity grew out of shared values and politics as well as the shared personal experience of our search for a place to do our work, for an intellectual and political community we could call home. Our identity as a group was also formed around the shared themes, methodologies, and voices that were emerging in our work.

We turned to new approaches. Borrowing from and critiquing other intellectual traditions, including liberalism, Marxism, the law and society movement, critical legal studies, feminism, poststructuralism/postmodernism, and neopragmatism, we began examining the relationships between naming and reality, knowledge and power. We examined the role of liberal-capitalist ideology in maintaining an unjust racial status quo and the role of narrow legal definitions of merit, fault, and causation in advancing or impairing the search for racial justice. We identified majoritarian self-interest as a critical factor in the ebb and flow of civil rights doctrine and demonstrated how areas of law ostensibly designed to advance the cause of racial equality often benefit powerful whites more than those who are racially oppressed. Our work presented racism not as isolated instances of conscious bigoted decisionmaking or prejudiced practice, but as larger, systemic, structural, and cultural, as deeply psychologically and socially ingrained.

New forms of scholarship began to emerge. We used personal histories, parables, chronicles, dreams, stories, poetry, fiction, and revisionist histories to convey our message. We called for greater attention to questions of audience—for whom were we writing and why? None of these methods was unique to our work, but their frequent use by scholars of color as a part of a race-centered enterprise indicated the emergence of a genre or movement. It was this 1980s generation of liberation scholarship that came to be known as critical race theory.

In a search for a tentative expository answer to the question "What is critical race theory?" critical race scholars have identified the following defining elements:

1. Critical race theory recognizes that racism is endemic to American life. Thus, the question for us is not so much whether or how racial discrimination can be eliminated while maintaining the integrity of other interests implicated in the status quo such as federalism, privacy, traditional values, or established property interests. Instead we ask how these traditional interests and values serve as vessels of racial subordination.

2. Critical race theory expresses skepticism toward dominant legal claims of neutrality, objectivity, color blindness, and meritocracy. These claims are central to an ideology of equal opportunity that presents race as an immutable characteristic devoid of social meaning and tells an ahistorical, abstracted story of racial inequality as a series of randomly occurring, intentional, and individualized acts.

3. Critical race theory challenges ahistoricism and insists on a contextual/historical analysis of the law. Current inequalities and social/institutional practices are linked to earlier periods in which the intent and cultural meaning of such practices were clear. More important, as critical race theorists we adopt a stance that presumes that racism has contributed to all contemporary manifestations of group advantage and disadvantage along racial lines, including differences in income, imprisonment, health, housing, education, political representation, and military service. Our history calls for this presumption.

4. Critical race theory insists on recognition of the experiential knowledge of people of color and our communities of origin in analyzing law and society. This knowledge is gained from critical reflection on the lived experience of racism and from critical reflection upon active political practice toward the elimination of racism.

5. Critical race theory is interdisciplinary and eclectic. It borrows from several traditions, including liberalism, law and society, feminism, Marxism, poststructuralism, critical legal theory, pragmatism, and nationalism. This eclecticism allows critical race theory to examine and incorporate those aspects of a methodology or theory that effectively enable our voice and advance the cause of racial justice even as we maintain a critical posture.

6. Critical race theory works toward the end of eliminating racial oppression as part of the broader goal of ending all forms of oppression. Racial oppression is experienced by many in tandem with oppression on grounds of gender, class, or sexual orientation. Critical race theory measures progress by a yardstick that looks to fundamental social

transformation. The interests of all people of color necessarily require not just adjustments within the established hierarchies, but a challenge to hierarchy itself. This recognition of intersecting forms of subordination requires multiple consciousness and political practices that address the varied ways in which people experience subordination.

Critical Race Scholars Enter the First Amendment Debate

How is it that the four authors whose essays appear in this book have found themselves at the center of the debate on assaultive speech? What has drawn us to this work? How has our identity and our political identification shaped the way we think about the first amendment?

Our entry into the contemporary discourse on assaultive speech and the first amendment is impelled and informed by the practice of liberationist pedagogy and by the emerging discipline of critical race theory. We joined this dialogue at different times and places. We focus on different aspects of this complex problem and suggest different solutions, but all of the work in this book is part of a larger project that we share. All of us found ourselves increasingly drawn into writing, speaking, and engaging in public debate as incidents of assaultive speech increased in recent years. We did not enter this debate to demonstrate our skill at intellectual swordplay. Nor did we become involved because it had become a faddish hot topic. Assaultive speech directly affected our lives and the lives of people for whom we cared: family, friends, students, and colleagues.

Our work is a pragmatic response to the urgent needs of students of color and other victims of hate speech who are daily silenced, intimidated, and subjected to severe psychological and physical trauma by racist assailants who employ words and symbols as part of an integrated arsenal of weapons of oppression and subordination. Students at Stanford, at the universities of Wisconsin and Michigan, at Duke and Yale and UCLA needed protection from the most flagrant forms of verbal abuse so that they could attend to their schoolwork. Political organizers in Detroit and Alabama, working men and women breaking color and gender barriers in factories and police forces, needed to have their stories told. Our colleagues of color, struggling to carry the multiple burdens of token representative, role model, and change agent in increasingly hostile environments, needed to know that the institutions in which they worked stood behind them.

Each of us knew that we were inclined to be more cautious, less outspoken and visible, after a rash of hate tracts had appeared in our mail or been stuffed under our doors. We knew that we walked more quickly to our cars after late nights at the office and glanced more often over our shoulders as we jogged the trails around our campuses. We needed theory and analysis to articulate and explain our reality, to deconstruct the theories that did not take our experience into account, to let us know that we were not crazy, to make a space for our voices in the debate.

For example, Charles Lawrence's chapter "If He Hollers Let Him Go: Regulating Racist Speech on Campus," began as an effort to articulate the injury and exclusion experienced by Black students at Stanford in the wake of what became known as the Ujamaa incident.[3]

Two white freshmen had defaced a poster bearing the likeness of Beethoven. They had colored the drawing of Beethoven brown, given it wild curly hair, big lips, and red eyes, and posted it on the door of an African-American student's dorm room in Ujamaa, the Black theme house. The two white students involved had been in an argument with the Black student the night before. They had contested the Black student's assertion that Beethoven was of African descent. Another poster, advertising a Black fraternity dance, was also found defaced on the dorm bulletin board. The word "niggers" had been written in large letters across the face of the poster. After investigating the incident the university's office of general counsel held that the offending students could not be disciplined under the university's disciplinary rules because their actions constituted protected speech.

The immediate reaction of many white students and faculty on campus to the Ujamaa incident was to treat it as an unfortunate boyish prank by misguided undergraduates. They could not understand the intensity of the strong emotional reaction by Black students. They saw the incident as unique, as unrepresentative of the racial climate at Stanford, and as a relatively mild example of the kind of racial harassment that was becoming increasingly common on American campuses. Surely, they argued, the danger to free speech and intellectual debate that would result from punishing speech of this sort counseled tolerance of this isolated case. The Black students' call for regulations was the worst kind of censorship. Hadn't they learned about the first amendment?

Lawrence experienced the incident very differently. The Sambo-like caricature drawn on the poster injured him quite directly. It was not an injury to an unknown other. Upon first hearing of it, he felt the blow of its message. The message said, "This is you. This is you and all of your African-American brothers and sisters. You are all Sambos. It's a joke to think that you could ever be a Beethoven. It's ridiculous to believe that you could ever be anything other than a caricature of real genius."

The clarity of this message, the painful impact of its blow, was the genesis of legal theory. This was injury to a group. To privatize it ignored the greatest part of the injury. The power of the poster's message was derived from its historical and cultural context, from the background of minstrel shows, of racist theories about brain size and gene pools and biblical ancestors that has shaped our conscious and unconscious beliefs about the intellectual capacity of Blacks. Without that context the defacement had no meaning. Moreover, the intent and impact of this message was to end discussion, not to continue it. It was not a rebuttal to the substance of the Black student's argument. It was an attack on his standing to engage in intellectual exchange.

Lawrence experienced the defacement as representative of the university community's racism and not as an exceptional incident in a community in which the absence of racism is the rule. As a token Black faculty member at Stanford, he had heard many stories from victims of hate speech that went unreported and unheard by his white colleagues. These were stories he'd heard throughout his life. He had been the target himself more times than he could count.

In considering how best to frame an analysis that might serve students and colleagues of color seeking to be heard in a debate framed by his white colleagues as one concerning the threat posed by censorship to academic freedom, Lawrence placed race at the center of his analysis. His first and ultimate inquiry was how the analysis advanced or hindered the goal of eliminating racial oppression and other mutually reinforcing forms of subordination.

It was this methodology that led him to see *Brown v. Board of Education* as a case about the nature of the injury of hate speech. In recognizing the inherent unconstitutionality of segregation, the Supreme Court identified the defamatory symbolism of segregation as central to its unconstitutionality and showed that racism achieves its purpose by the construction of meaning. As the critical race scholar Kendall Thomas says, "We are raced." We are acted upon and constructed by racist speech. The meaning of "Black" or "white" is derived through a history of acted-upon ideology.

It was this methodology that led Mari Matsuda to antisubordination as the guiding principle to determine when hate speech is antithetical to the underlying liberal democratic principles that inform both the first amendment and the equal protection clause. In "Public Response to Racist Speech: Considering the Victim's Story," Matsuda asks that we listen first to the voices of the victims of hate speech. She is not content simply to tell the victim's story. Their liberation must be the bottom line of any first amendment analysis.

Matsuda's work is influenced by the use of narrative and the authority of personal experience that characterizes strands of both feminist thought and critical race theory. In developing her analysis of hate speech and the first amendment, she spoke with students at universities throughout the country and worked with community groups involved in antiracist struggle. The connection between hate speech and violence, and loss of liberty experienced by targets of hate speech, compelled her to confront the contradiction between first amendment absolutism and the goals of liberty and equality.

Matsuda's parents were labor and civil rights activists who paid a price for their unpopular beliefs during the McCarthy period. Censorship, blacklisting, and intimidation affected her family in a concrete way. Mindful of this experience, Matsuda draws a distinction between dissent—or the right to criticize the powerful institutions that govern our lives—and hate speech, which is directed against the least powerful segments of our community. This distinction, Matsuda argues, is a principled one, given the historical contexts of subordination that she uses as a starting point for developing legal theory.

Likewise it is the methodology of critical race theory that prompted Kimberlè Crenshaw to examine the intersectionality of race and gender subordination in the alarming incidence of violence against women of color and to ask about the role that speech, or the representation of women of color in mass culture, plays in constructing the unique combinations of racism and patriarchy that limit and endanger the lives of women of color. In examining the obscenity prosecution of the Black rap group 2 Live Crew, Crenshaw found herself torn between defending these three Black men against the racist attack of selective prosecution and opposing the frightening explosion of violent imagery against Black women that was represented in their music. Faced with the question of how to construct a Black feminist approach to the virulent misogyny of 2 Live Crew, Crenshaw saw the need to understand the larger issue of gender violence. "Beyond Racism and Misogyny: Black Feminism and 2 Live Crew" explores the ways in which the politics and discourse of race and gender have worked to exclude and marginalize women of color. It is an example of the critical race theorist revealing the connections between representational, political, and material dynamics of subordination. Crenshaw takes a case that came to the courts as a case about free speech and shows us that much more is at stake than whether 2 Live Crew's album *As Nasty As They Wanna Be* is protected by the first amendment.

Richard Delgado's "Words That Wound: A Tort Action for Racial Insults, Epithets, and Name Calling" was the first article to explore the injuries inflicted by racist hate speech and the potential tensions between legal remedies for those injuries and the first amendment. This pathbreaking article was first published in 1982 when critical race theory was still in its infancy. But Delgado's use of cases to graphically portray the injury; his use of psychology, sociology, and political theory to explain the nature of the harm; and his exploration of common law doctrine that was moving toward providing a pragmatic remedy for those suffering from racial subordination foreshadowed the methodology that critical race theorists later sought to define and name. Delgado pointed out that values central to the first amendment itself were subverted by racist speech and identified racism as the reason for such selective disregard.

Building Theory Through Reflection on Action

Central to the methodology of critical race theory and liberationist pedagogy is an ongoing engagement in political practice. The Brazilian educator and philosopher Paulo Freire has said that liberationist teaching contains two dimensions, "Reflection and action, in such radical interaction that if one is sacrificed—even in part—the other immediately suffers."[4] In our work on hate speech and the first amendment we have sought to follow this precept, seeking always to inform our understanding and analysis by critical reflection on political action.

This continuing search means that the positions reflected in these essays are contingent, not static. Our work has been shaped and continues to be shaped in the crucible of dialogue, debate, consciousness raising, and political struggle. As we have traveled around the country giving speeches, participating on panels, listening to students, and consulting with community activists, faculties, administrators, legislators, and judges, we have continued to learn much about the nature of this political project. We have learned that even as we understand and name the world we see, it changes and must be understood and named again. This introduction would not be complete without some discussion of audience. To whom have we been speaking? What have been the range of responses to our work and what are the tentative understandings we have gained from those responses?

First amendment hard-liners have been our most vocal and most predictable audience. Political pundits across the political spectrum from George Will to Nat Hentoff have attacked our efforts as the work of "thought police," "leftist censors," and "first amendment revisionists." The attention that these more inflammatory and contentious attacks have received in the media has meant that we have spent a great deal of our time and energy responding to the position of these first amendment fundamentalists. The articles in this book answer in some detail the questions most frequently put by those who adhere to the absolutist or near-absolutist position that any regulation of assaultive speech is too much. Lawrence reflects on the source of these first amendment fundamentalists' resistance to even narrowly framed regulations of hate speech in contexts in which the courts have already permitted the regulation of expression. Noting that there are already many places in first amendment law in which competing interests such as privacy, individual reputation, protection of intellectual property, and regulation of economic markets are judged to justify infringements on speech, he asks if the reluctance to regulate hate speech is related to unconscious racism.

Although the civil liberties community is deeply ambivalent about this difficult set of issues, we have found that many confirmed civil libertarians are open to our ideas and that the narratives and analyses contained within this book have convinced many of them to move away from a more absolutist position. The 1989 biennial conference of the ACLU devoted a plenary session and two days of debate to the issues raised in these essays, and two years later the national board of the ACLU issued a policy statement that reflected a new sensitivity to the harm that assaultive speech may do to both its victims and to the political discourse we seek to protect with the first amendment. Those individuals in our audience who read and listen to our work and find themselves questioning previously held assumptions are testimony to the power of story telling and cross-cultural translation that is central to critical race theory and liberation pedagogy.

Perhaps our most important audience has been the community of individuals who are the victims of subordinating speech—people of color, Jews, women, gay men, and lesbians—who are regularly subjected to taunts and threats. Matsuda describes the beginnings of her insights into the pervasive injury done by sexual harassment and assaultive speech as follows:

> Five years ago I began speaking to university and community groups about sexual harassment. An eerie pattern emerged in these speaking forays. After I would give my talk about the legal analysis of sexual harassment, throwing in a little bit of feminist theory and answering a predictable array of questions about what is and what isn't sexual harassment, I would conclude and prepare to leave. The crowd would thin out, and a woman would remain on its edges, waiting to talk to me. When she was certain the others were out of hearing range, she would come up to me and say, in a voice both guilty and grateful for the chance to speak, "It happened to me." Secretaries told me of bosses who chased them around desks—men they were afraid to be in elevators with, jobs they'd had to leave because "he couldn't keep his hands off me." Students told me of professors who would call them into the office for special conferences that turned out to be sexual propositions. I heard these stories regularly about the downtown law firms, about the beautiful campus where I work. Suddenly the elegant offices, the broad, tree-lined walkways of my university looked different, because underneath the appearance of normalcy, I came to see an epidemic of hateful behavior toward women. Students would call me anonymously to tell me harassment stories rich with the kind of detail that comes from truth. A therapist wrote to me to tell me of her patient, date-raped by a colleague. I learned the techniques of the academic harasser, how particularly adept some of them are at exploiting the student's wishes for more intimate contact in a large university, how the antihierarchy of phony liberalism is used to confuse students about the limits of appropriate intimacy in academic relationships.
>
> As I heard these stories, as I heard from women who had left school, who had gone into therapy, who blamed themselves for the aggression of others, I perceived an emergency, appropriately responded to by regulations against sexual harassment. To my surprise, many of my colleagues disagreed. Rules against sexual harassment, particularly rules against so-called voluntary sexual relations between students and faculty, were seen as violations of academic freedom and personal choice. Women have to toughen up, I was told. They need to stop thinking like victims and learn to stand up to harassers. Regulations against harassment could lead to a chilling effect, preventing warm student-teacher relations. Proposals for regulations were antisex, antilove, authoritarian, and violative of basic civil liberties.
>
> In the meantime, I was also researching and writing on the topic of racist speech and traveling to various universities making legal arguments that are

viewed as heresy by many civil libertarians. I argued for narrow restriction of racist speech because of its impact on victims. At every single university at which I spoke—north, south, east, and west—I learned of serious incidents of racist or anti-Semitic assault. University administrators reported that they had never seen anything like it. A pattern emerged in the 1980s of the new integration colliding with the new racism—or the new old racism. The universities—long the home of institutional and euphemistic racism—were now seeing something different: the worst forms of gutter racism. Swastikas appearing on Jewish holy days, cross burnings, racist slurs, and verbal assaults so degrading and vicious I found I could not reprint some of them, even for educational purposes, in the article I wrote.[5]

Too often victims of hate speech find themselves without the words to articulate what they see, feel, and know. In the absence of theory and analysis that give them a diagnosis and a name for the injury they have suffered, they internalize the injury done them and are rendered silent in the face of continuing injury. Critical race theory names the injury and identifies its origins, origins that are often well disguised in the rhetoric of shared values and neutral legal principles. When ideology is deconstructed and injury is named, subordinated victims find their voices. They discover they are not alone in their subordination. They are empowered. This empowerment, this helping others to find their voices as we find our own, is the most important part of our work.

The political education that is gained in the debate itself—participants hearing their own stories and the stories of others, hearing the arguments framed and learning to make them themselves—is what gives new strength to embattled students and political activists. This, more than getting a university to adopt a regulation or changing the thinking of first amendment fundamentalists, is the work that must be done.

Toward a Postcolonial University: Reflections on the Right to Be Racist

One of the things that we have discovered as we engage in the debate over hate speech and the first amendment is that we often find ourselves in familiar intellectual territory. We hear ourselves making arguments we have made before, in other settings and with reference to other legal issues. We find ourselves echoing themes that were introduced in our work on school desegregation, affirmative action, reparations, religious freedom, and legal history. This sense of déjà vu, this experience of traveling an often-traveled terrain, is not coincidental. It reflects the grounding of our work in lived experience and political purpose. It is inevitable that our work on the first amendment brings us to intellectual and political crossroads we have come to before, because these intersections are found on the path that defines the tradition and practice of radical teaching that we have chosen as our own.

One of these intersections bears special mention in this introduction. This is the reemerging debate over affirmative action and the meaning of diversity within our colleges and universities. Contemporaneous with the recent outbreak of gutter hate speech and racial harassment, there is an emerging and increasingly virulent backlash against the extremely modest successes achieved by communities of color, women, and other subordinated groups in our efforts to integrate academic institutions run by and for white male elites. The chief spokespersons for this more refined sentiment against persons and voices that are new and unfamiliar to the campus and intellectual discourse are not the purveyors of gutter hate speech. They are polite and polished colleagues. The code words of this backlash are words like merit, rigor, standards, qualifications, and excellence. Increasingly we hear those who are resisting change appropriating the language of freedom struggles. Words like intolerant, silencing, McCarthyism, censors, and orthodoxy are used to portray women and people of color as oppressors and to pretend that the powerful have become powerless.

These colleagues mourn the passing of an era when we "all" read the "great books," when we knew what it meant to be an "educated man," and when we were not afraid to require our students and colleagues to meet that standard. They call for the reinstitution of compulsory courses on "Western Civilization" and resist the inclusion of significant non-European or women's writings in those courses. They are profoundly critical of any effort to change the composition of the academic community or the content of the intellectual discourse by giving attention to the race or gender of potential participants.

We have been fighting this battle over affirmative action, multiculturalism, the meaning of merit, and the inclusion of historically excluded persons and voices for all of our professional lives. The struggle against institutional, structural, and culturally ingrained unconscious racism and the movement toward a fully multicultural, postcolonial university is central to the work of the liberationist teacher. This is at bottom a fight to gain equal access to the power of the intelligentsia to construct knowledge, social meaning, ideology, and definitions of who "we" are.

Now the defenders of the status quo have discovered, in the first amendment, a new weapon. The debate about affirmative action and the inclusion of historically excluded groups is being recast as a debate about free speech. We have begun to hear a rhetoric from those of our colleagues who are most fearful of change that sounds much like what we hear from first amendment fundamentalists: Arguments for absolutist protection of speech made without reference to historical context or uneven power relations. Academic freedom and intellectual pursuit are alleged to be threatened by "leftist speech police." People of color, women, gays, and lesbians who insist on the inclusion of their voices in academic discourse and who speak out against persons and practices that continue to injure and demean them are said to impose a "new orthodoxy" upon the academy. Tenured professors say that they are afraid to raise controversial issues, use humor in their classes, or express friendliness toward their students for fear of being called a racist, a sexist, or a homophobe by "oversensitive" students.

Stripped of its context this is a seductive argument. The privilege and power of white male elites is wrapped in the rhetoric of politically unpopular speech. Those with the power to exclude new voices from the official canon become an oppressed minority. Academic freedom to express one's beliefs is decontextualized from the speaker's power to impose those beliefs on others. The isolated Black, Brown, or Asian faculty member, the small group of students who risk future careers in raising their voices against racism, are cast as powerful censors.

The first amendment arms conscious and unconscious racists—Nazis and liberals alike—with a constitutional right to be racist. Racism is just another idea deserving of constitutional protection like all ideas. The first amendment is employed to trump or nullify the only substantive meaning of the equal protection clause, that the Constitution mandates the disestablishment of the ideology of racism.

What is ultimately at stake in this debate is our vision for this society. We are in this fight about the first amendment because it is more than a fight about how to balance one individual's freedom of speech against another individual's freedom from injury. This is a fight about the substantive content that we will give to the ideals of freedom and equality—how we will construct "freedom," as a constitutional premise and a defining principle of democracy.

This is the same fight that is the subject of all of our work. It is a fight for a vision of society where the substance of freedom is freedom from degradation, humiliation, battering, starvation, homelessness, hopelessness, and other forms of violence to the person that deny one's full humanity. It is a fight for a constitutional community where "freedom" does not implicate a right to degrade and humiliate another human being any more than it implicates a right to do physical violence to another or a right to enslave another or a right to economically exploit another in a sweatshop, in a coal mine, or in the fields.

In this book we use the words of law and politics to fight the words that wound and exclude. We seek a legal system that recognizes and remedies the harm of the structures of have and have-not, and we express our solidarity with all who join us in that quest.

2

Public Response to Racist Speech: Considering the Victim's Story

Mari J. Matsuda

A Black family enters a coffee shop in a small Texas town. A white man places a card on their table. The card reads, "You have just been paid a visit by the Ku Klux Klan." The family stands and leaves.[1]

A law student goes to her dorm and finds an anonymous message posted on the door, a caricature image of her race, with a red line slashed through it.[2]

A Japanese-American professor arrives in an Australian city and finds a proliferation of posters stating "Asians Out or Racial War" displayed on telephone poles. She uses her best, educated inflection in speaking with clerks and cab drivers and decides not to complain when she is overcharged.[3]

These unheralded stories share company with the more notorious provocation of swastikas at Skokie, Illinois, and burning crosses on suburban lawns. The threat of hate groups like the Ku Klux Klan and the neo-Nazi skinheads goes beyond their repeated acts of illegal violence. Their presence and the active dissemination of racist propaganda means that citizens are denied personal security and liberty as they go about their daily lives. Richard Delgado recognizes the harm of racist speech in Chapter 4 of this book, suggesting a tort remedy for injury from racist words. Taking inspiration from Delgado's position, I make the further suggestion that formal criminal and administrative sanction—public as opposed to private prosecution—is also an appropriate response to racist speech.

Chapter 2 moves between two stories. The first is the victim's story of the effects of racist hate messages. The second is the first amendment story of free speech. The intent is to respect and value both stories. This bipolar discourse uses as its method what many outsider intellectuals do in silence: it mediates between different ways of knowing to determine what is true and what is just.

17

In calling for legal sanctions for racist speech, this chapter rejects an absolutist first amendment position. It calls for movement of the societal response to racist speech from the private to the public realm. The choice of public sanction, enforced by the state, is a significant one. The kinds of injuries historically left to private individuals to absorb and resist through private means are no accident. The places where the law does not go to redress harm have tended to be the places where women, children, people of color, and poor people live. This absence of law is itself another story with a message, perhaps unintended, about the relative value of different human lives. A legal response to racist speech is a statement that victims of racism are valued members of our polity.

The call for a formal, legal-structural response to racist speech goes against the long-standing and healthy American distrust of government power. It goes against an American tradition of tolerance that is precious in the sense of being both valuable and fragile.

Lee Bollinger, dean of the University of Michigan Law School, has concluded that a primary reason for the legal protection of hate speech is to reinforce our commitment to tolerance as a value.[4] If we can shore up our commitment to free speech in the hard and public cases, like *Skokie*,[5] perhaps we will internalize the need for tolerance and spare ourselves from regrettable error in times of stress. Given the real historical costs of state intolerance of minority views, the first amendment purpose Bollinger identifies is not one lightly set aside.

Recognizing both the real harm of racist speech and the need to strengthen our dangerously fickle collective commitment to freedom of discourse, I intend to feel and to work within the first amendment tension armed with stories from human lives. This chapter suggests that outsider jurisprudence— jurisprudence derived from considering stories from the bottom—will help resolve the seemingly irresolvable conflicts of value and doctrine that characterize liberal thought. I conclude that an absolutist first amendment response to hate speech has the effect of perpetuating racism: Tolerance of hate speech is not tolerance borne by the community at large. Rather, it is a psychic tax imposed on those least able to pay.

Outsider Jurisprudence

If we cannot understand this pain that women, that Indian women, that Black women, that Hawaiian women, that Chicano women go through, we are never going to understand anything. All the mega-theory will not get us anywhere because without that understanding, mega-theory does not mean anything, does not reflect social reality, does not reflect people's experience.

—Patricia Monture[6]

There is an outsider's jurisprudence growing and thriving alongside mainstream jurisprudence in American law schools. The new feminist jurisprudence is a lively example of this. A related, and less celebrated, outsider jurisprudence is that belonging to people of color.

Critical race theorists tend to use a methodology grounded in the particulars of their social reality and experience. This method is consciously both historical and revisionist, attempting to know history from the bottom. From the fear and namelessness of the slave, from the broken treaties of the indigenous Americans, the desire to know history from the bottom has forced these scholars to sources often ignored: journals, poems, oral histories, and stories from their own experiences of life in a hierarchically arranged world.

This methodology, which rejects presentist, androcentric, Eurocentric, and falsely universalist descriptions of social phenomena, offers a unique description of law. The description is realist, but not necessarily nihilist. It accepts the standard teaching of street wisdom: Law is essentially political. It accepts as well the pragmatic use of law as a tool for social change and the aspirational core of law as the human dream of peaceable existence. If these views seem contradictory, that is consistent with another component of jurisprudence of color: It is jurisprudence recognizing, struggling within, and utilizing contradiction, dualism, and ambiguity.

The senior critical race theorist Derrick Bell's book *And We Are Not Saved*[7] is an example of this methodology. Bell describes a world infused with racism. This description ties law to racism, showing that law is both a product and a promoter of racism. Like the feminists who have shown that patriarchy has had its own march through history, related to but distinct from the march of class struggle, scholars of color have shown how racism is a separate, distinct, and central phenomenon in American life.

The hopeful part of the description offered by theorists such as Bell is the occasional recognition of the vulnerability of racist structures. The few who have managed to subject the many to conditions of degradation have used a variety of devices, from genocide to liberal doublespeak, that reveal the deep contradictions and instability inherent in any organization of social life dependent upon subordination. The sorrow songs of the critical race theorists are thus tempered by an underlying descriptive message of the inevitability of humane social progress.

This progress can lead to a just world free of existing conditions of domination. The prescriptive message of outsider jurisprudence offers signposts to guide our way there: the focus on effects. The need to attack the effects of racism and patriarchy in order to attack the deep, hidden, tangled roots characterizes outsider thinking about law. Outsiders thus search for what Anne Scales has called the rachet—legal tools that have progressive effect, defying the habit of neutral principles to entrench existing power. Outsider scholars have derived rachetlike measures to eliminate effects of oppression, including affirmative action, reparations, desegregation, and the criminalization of racist and misogynist propaganda. Such measures are best implemented through formal rules, formal procedures, and formal concepts of rights, for informality and oppression are frequent fellow travelers. Although cognizant of the limits of law reform, outsider scholars have emphasized the instrumental uses of formal legal rules to achieve substantive justice.

Using the descriptive and prescriptive messages of the emerging outsider jurisprudence to confront the problem of racist hate messages provides new insights into the long-standing neutral-principle dilemma of liberal jurisprudence. The following section will show how the victim's story illuminates particular values and suggests particular solutions to the problem of racist hate messages.

Racist Hate Messages: The Victim's Story

The attempt to split bias from violence has been this society's most enduring rationalization.

—Patricia Williams[8]

Who Sees What: Some Initial Stories

In writing this chapter I am forced to ask why the world looks so different to me from the way it looks to many of the civil libertarians whom I consider my allies. Classical thought labels ad hominem analysis a logical fallacy. The identity of the person doing the analysis often seems to make the difference, however, in responding to racist speech. In advocating legal restriction of hate speech, I have found my most sympathetic audience in people who identify with target groups, whereas I have often encountered incredulity, skepticism, and even hostility from others.

This split in reaction is also evident in case studies of hate speech. The typical reaction of target-group members to an incident of racist propaganda is alarm and immediate calls for redress. The typical reaction of non-members is to consider the incidents isolated pranks, the product of sick but harmless minds. This is in part a defensive reaction: a refusal to believe that real people, people just like us, are racists. This disassociation leads logically to the claim that there is no institutional or state responsibility to respond to the incident. It is not the kind of real and pervasive threat that requires the state's power to quell.

Here are some true "just kidding" stories:

An African-American worker found himself repeatedly subjected to racist speech when he came to work. A noose was hanging one day in his work area; a dead animal and other threatening objects were placed in his locker. "KKK" references were directed at him, as well as other racist slurs and death threats. His employer discouraged him from calling the police, attributing the incidents to "horseplay."[9]

In San Francisco, a swastika was placed near the desks of Asian-American and African-American inspectors in the newly integrated fire department. The official explanation for the presence of the swastika at the fire department was that it was presented several years earlier as a "joke" gift to the battalion chief, and that it was unclear why or how it ended up at the work stations of the minority employees.[10]

In Jackson, Mississippi, African-American employees of Frito-Lay found their cars sprayed with "KKK" inscriptions and were the targets of racist notes and threats. Local African Americans and Jews were concerned, but officials said the incidents were attributable to children.[11]

An African-American FBI agent was subject to a campaign of racist taunts by white coworkers. A picture of an ape was pasted over his child's photograph, and racial slurs were used. Such incidents were called "healthy" by his supervisor.[12]

In Seattle, a middle-management Japanese American was disturbed by his employer's new anti-Japanese campaign. As the employer's use of slurs and racist slogans in the workplace increased, so did the employee's discomfort. His objections were viewed as overly sensitive and uncooperative. He finally quit his job, and he was denied unemployment insurance benefits because his departure was "without cause."[13]

In Contra Costa County, California, Ku Klux Klan symbols were used to turn families looking for homes away from certain neighborhoods. The local sheriff said there was "nothing . . . to indicate this is Klan activity."[14]

Similarly, a Hmong family in Eureka, California, was twice victimized by four-foot-high crosses burning on their lawn. Local police dismissed this as "a prank."[15]

Why might anti-Japanese racial slurs mean something different to Asian and white managers? Here is a story of mine:

As a young child I was told never to let anyone call me a J—p. My parents, normally peaceable and indulgent folk, told me this in the tone reserved for dead-serious warnings. Don't accept rides from strangers. Don't play with matches. Don't let anyone call you that name. In their tone they transmitted a message of danger, that the word was a dangerous one, tied to violence.

Just as I grew up to learn the facts about the unspoken danger my parents saw in the stranger in the car, I learned how they connected the violence of California lynch mobs and Hiroshima atom bombs to racist slurs against Japanese Americans.

This early training in vigilance was reinforced by what I later learned about violence and Asian Americans: that people with features like mine are regular victims of violence tied to a wave of anti-Asian propaganda that stretches from Boston to San Francisco, from Galveston to Detroit.

The white managers who considered Mr. O. (the Japanese-American manager) an overly sensitive troublemaker and the unemployment board that determined there was no good cause for him to quit his job came from a different experience. They probably never heard of Vincent Chin, a twenty-seven-year-old Chinese American beaten to death by thugs wielding baseball bats who yelled, "It's because of you fucking J—ps that we're out of work!" They do not know about the Southeast-Asian–American children spat upon and taunted as they walk home from school in Boston; about the vigilante patrols harassing Vietnamese shrimpers in Texas. Nor do they know that the violence in all these cases is preceded by propaganda similar to that used in Mr. O.'s workplace: that those [racist slur for Asian groups] are taking over "our" country.

Stories of anti-Asian violence are regularly reported in the Asian-American press; just as stories of synagogue vandalism are regularly reported in the Jewish-American press; and anti–African-American violence, including the all-too-common phenomenon of "move-in" violence, is regularly reported in the African-American press. Members of target-group communities tend to know that racial violence and harassment are widespread, common, and life threatening; that, as one Georgia observer put it, "The youngsters who paint a swastika today may throw a bomb tomorrow."[16]

The mainstream press often ignores these stories, giving rise to the view of racist and anti-Semitic incidents as random and isolated and the corollary that isolated incidents are inconsequential. For informed members of the victim communities, however, it is logical to link together several thousand real-life stories into one tale of caution.

The Structure of Racism

Although this chapter focuses on the phenomenology of racism, it includes a discussion of the closely related phenomenon of anti-Semitism. The same groups, using many of the same techniques and operating from many of the same motivations and dysfunctions, typically produce racist and anti-Semitic speech. The serious problems of violent pornography and antigay and antilesbian hate speech are not the focus here. Although I believe these forms of hate speech require public restriction, these forms also require a separate analysis because of the complex and violent nature of gender subordination and the different way in which sex operates as a locus of oppression. The deadly violence that accompanies the persistent verbal degradation of those subordinated because of gender or sexuality explodes the notion that there are clear lines between words and deeds. In considering the emerging theory that patriarchy and heterosexism are cornerstones of violence in our society, I note that in researching hundreds of incidents of racist violence in preparation for this chapter, I found in virtually every case the perpetrators were men. Thus although the focus of this chapter is racist speech, other forms of subordination are always, uneasily close at hand.

The claim that a legal response to racist speech is required stems from a recognition of the structural reality of racism in the United States. Racism, as used here, comprises the ideology of racial supremacy and the mechanisms for keeping selected victim groups in subordinated positions. The implements of racism include:

1. Violence and genocide,
2. Racial hate messages, disparagement, and threats
3. Overt disparate treatment
4. Covert disparate treatment and sanitized racist comments ,

In addition to physical violence, there is what the legal scholar Robert Cover called the violence of the word.[17] Racist hate messages, threats, slurs, epithets, and disparagement all hit the gut of those in the target group. The spoken message of hatred and inferiority is conveyed on the street, in school yards, in popular culture, and in the propaganda of hate widely distributed in this country. Our college campuses have seen an epidemic of racist incidents since the early 1980s. The hate speech flaring up in our midst includes insulting nouns for racial groups, degrading caricatures, threats of violence, and literature portraying Jews and people of color as animal-like and requiring extermination.

Although violence and hate propaganda are officially renounced by elites, other forms of racism are not. Jim Crow, which persists today in the form of private clubs and de facto segregated schools and neighborhoods, is seen as less offensive than cross burnings. Covert disparate treatment and sanitized racist comments are commonplace and socially acceptable in many settings. The various implements of racism find their way into the hands of different dominant-group members. Lower- and middle-class white men might use violence against people of color, whereas upper-class whites might resort to private clubs or righteous indignation against "diversity" and "reverse discrimination." Institutions—government bodies, schools, corporations—also perpetuate racism through a variety of overt and covert means.

From the victim's perspective, all of these implements inflict wounds,

wounds that are neither random nor isolated. Gutter racism, parlor racism, corporate racism, and government racism work in coordination, reinforcing existing conditions of domination. Less egregious forms of racism degenerate easily into more serious forms.

The Japanese-American executive who resigns in protest when his employer starts publishing anti-Japanese slogans to improve sales knows that there is a connection between racist words and racist deeds. The racially motivated beating death of Vincent Chin by unemployed white auto workers in Detroit, during a time of widespread anti-Asian propaganda in the auto industry, was no accident. Nor was the murder of the Davis, California, high school student Thong Hy Huynh, after months of anti-Asian racial slurs.

Violence is a necessary and inevitable part of the structure of racism. It is the final solution, as fascists know, barely held at bay while the tactical weapons of segregation, disparagement, and hate propaganda do their work. The historical connection of all the tools of racism is a record against which to consider a legal response to racist speech.

The Specific Negative Effects of Racist Hate Messages

> *everywhere the crosses are burning,*
> *sharp-shooting goose-steppers around every corner,*
> *there are snipers in the schools . . .*
> *(I know you don't believe this.*
> *You think this is nothing*
> *but faddish exaggeration. But they*
> *are not shooting at you.)*

—Lorna Dee Cervantes[18]

Racist hate messages are rapidly increasing and are widely distributed in this country through a variety of low and high technologies, including anonymous phone calls and letters, posters, books, magazines and pamphlets, cable television, recorded phone messages, computer networks, bulk mail, graffiti, and leafleting. The negative effects of hate messages are real and immediate for the victims. Victims of vicious hate propaganda experience physiological symptoms and emotional distress ranging from fear in the gut to rapid pulse rate and difficulty in breathing, nightmares, post-traumatic stress disorder, hypertension, psychosis, and suicide. Patricia Williams has called the blow of racist messages "spirit murder" in recognition of the psychic destruction victims experience.[19]

Victims are restricted in their personal freedom. To avoid receiving hate messages, victims have to quit jobs, forgo education, leave their homes, avoid certain public places, curtail their own exercise of speech rights, and otherwise modify their behavior and demeanor. The recipient of hate messages struggles with inner turmoil. One subconscious response is to reject one's own identity as a victim-group member. As writers portraying the African-American experience have noted, the price of disassociating from one's own race is often sanity itself.

As much as one may try to resist a piece of hate propaganda, the effect on one's self-esteem and sense of personal security is devastating. To be hated, despised, and alone is the ultimate fear of all human beings. However irrational racist speech may be, it hits right at the emotional place where we feel the most pain. The aloneness comes not only from the hate message itself, but also from the government response of tolerance. When hundreds of police officers are called out to protect racist marchers, when the courts refuse redress for racial insult, and when racist attacks are officially dismissed as pranks, the victim becomes a stateless person. Target-group members must either identify with a community that promotes racist speech or admit that the community does not include them.

The effect on non–target-group members is also of constitutional dimensions. Associational and other liberty interests of whites are curtailed in an atmosphere rife with racial hatred. Hate messages, threats, and violence are often the price for whites of hiring, marrying, adopting, socializing with, and even jogging with people of color. In addition, the process of disassociation can affect the mental health of non-targets. Dominant-group members who rightfully, and often angrily, object to hate propaganda share a guilty secret: their relief that they are not themselves the target of the racist attack. Even as they reject the Ku Klux Klan, they may feel ambivalent relief that they are not African-American, Asian, or Jewish. Thus they are drawn into unwilling complicity with the Klan, spared from being the feared and degraded thing.

Just as when we confront human tragedy—a natural disaster, a plane crash—we feel the blessing of the fortunate that distances us from the victims, the presence of racist hate propaganda distances right-thinking dominant-group members from the victims, making it harder to achieve a sense of common humanity. Similarly, racist propaganda forces victim-group members to view all dominant-group members with suspicion. It forces well-meaning dominant-group members to use kid-glove care in dealing with outsiders. This is one reason why social relations across racial lines are so rare in the United States.

Research in the psychology of racism suggests a related effect of racist hate propaganda: At some level, no matter how much both victims and well-meaning dominant-group members resist it, racial inferiority is planted in our minds as an idea that may hold some truth.[20] The idea is improbable and abhorrent, but because it is presented repeatedly, it is there before us. "Those people" are lazy, dirty, sexualized, money grubbing, dishonest, inscrutable, we are told. We reject the idea, but the next time we sit next to one of "those people," the dirt message, the sex message, is triggered. We stifle it, reject it as wrong, but it is there, interfering with our perception and interaction with the person next to us. In conducting research for this chapter, I read an unhealthy number of racist statements. A few weeks after reading about a "dot busters" campaign against immigrants from India, I passed by an Indian woman on my campus. Instead of thinking, "What a beautiful sari," the first thought that came into my mind was "dot busters." Only after setting aside the hate message could I move on to my own thoughts. The propaganda I read had taken me one step back from casually treating a fellow brown-skinned human being as that, rather than as someone distanced from myself. For the victim, similarly, the angry rejection of the message of inferiority is coupled with absorption of the message. When a dominant-group member responds favorably, there is a moment of relief—the victims of hate messages do not always believe in their insides that they deserve decent treatment. This obsequious moment is degrading and dispiriting when the self-aware victim acknowledges it.

Psychologists and sociologists have done much to document the effects of racist messages on both victims and dominant-group members.[21] Writers of color have given us graphic portrayals of what life is like for victims of racist propaganda.[22] From the victim's perspective, racist hate messages cause real damage.

If the harm of racist hate messages is significant, and the truth value marginal, the doctrinal space for regulation of such speech becomes a possibility. An emerging international standard seizes this possibility.

International Law of Human Rights: The Emerging Acceptance of the Victim's Story

The international community has chosen to outlaw racist hate propaganda. Article 4 of the International Convention on the Elimination of All Forms of Racial Discrimination states:

State Parties condemn all propaganda and all organizations which are based on ideas or theories of superiority of one race or group of persons of one colour or ethnic origin, or which attempt to justify or promote racial hatred and discrimination in any form, and undertake to adopt immediate and positive measures designed to eradicate all incitement to, or acts of, such discrimination and, to this end, with due regard to the principles embodied in the Universal Declaration of Human Rights and the rights expressly set forth in Article 5 of this Convention, *inter alia:*

(*a*) Shall declare as an offence punishable by law all dissemination of ideas based on racial superiority or hatred, incitement to racial discrimination, as well as all acts of violence or incitement to such acts against any race or group of persons of another colour or ethnic origin, and also the provision of any assistance to racist activities, including the financing thereof;

(*b*) Shall declare illegal and prohibit organizations, and also organized and all other propaganda activities, which promote and incite racial discrimination, and shall recognize participation in such organization or activities as an offence punishable by law; [and]

(*c*) Shall not permit public authorities or public institutions, national or local, to promote or incite racial discrimination.[23]

Under this treaty, nation-states are required to criminalize racist hate messages. Prohibiting dissemination of ideas of racial superiority or hatred is not easily reconciled with U.S. concepts of free speech. The convention recognizes this conflict. Article 4 acknowledges the need for "due regard" for rights protected by the Universal Declaration of Human Rights and by Article 5 of the convention—including the rights of freedom of speech, association, and conscience.

Recognizing these conflicting values and nonetheless concluding that the right to freedom from racist hate propaganda deserves affirmative recognition represents the evolving international view. A U.S. lawyer, trained in a tradition of liberal thought, would read Article 4 and conclude immediately that it is unworkable. Acts of violence and perhaps imminent incitement to violence are properly prohibited, but the control of ideas is doomed to failure. This position was voiced continually in the debates preceding adoption of the convention,[24] leading to the view that Article 4 is both controversial and troublesome.

To those who struggled through early international attempts to deal with racist propaganda, the competing values carried a sense of urgency. The imagery of both book burnings and swastikas was clear in their minds. Hitler had banned ideas. He had also murdered six million Jews in the culmination of a campaign that had as a major theme the idea of racial superiority. Although the causes of fascism are complex, the knowledge that anti-Semitic hate propaganda and the rise of Nazism were clearly connected guided development of the emerging international law on incitement to racial hatred.

In 1959 and 1960, the world faced a resurgence of anti-Semitic incidents in several countries. The movement to implement the human rights goals of the UN Charter and the Universal Declaration of Human Rights gained momentum as member states sought effective means of eliminating discrimination.

Despite consensus on the basic goal of elimination of discrimination, there was division on the question of incitement to hatred. The Sub-Commission on the Prevention of Discrimination and Protection of Minorities began work in 1964, using three separate drafts prepared by representatives of the United States, the United Kingdom, and the USSR and Poland. Thus the sub-commission had the benefit of vastly different ideological views as well as a basic consensus on the necessity of combating discrimination.

In addressing incitement, the U.S. draft would have outlawed direct incitement to acts of racist violence.[25] It would have disallowed government involvement in chartering or supporting racist hate groups. This was consistent with U.S. constitutional principles. The USSR/Poland draft would have banned all "propaganda" of "superiority" and would have criminalized participation in any organization that discriminated or advocated discrimination.[26] In obvious contrast to the U.S. view, the socialist nations proposed direct action against hate messages, expressing little concern for an individualistic, civil libertarian conception of free speech.

Discussion by the Commission on Human Rights centered around the problems of proving when propaganda was likely to cause violence, and whether violence was the only end to avoid.[27] The problem of freedom of association and the banning of hate organizations was also discussed. The final decision, by a vote of sixteen in favor and five abstentions, was to adopt paragraph 4(b) as it is now written, banning propaganda activity that promoted discrimination and criminalizing participation in organizations promoting discrimination. The weaker U.S. position was thus rejected by the commission.

The proposed convention next went to the Third Committee of the General Assembly in 1965. Again the issues of the necessity of ties to violence and of recognition of free speech rights were raised. The United States proposed explicit recognition of the right of free speech within the text.[28] The committee chose instead to refer generally to "due regard" of such rights. Acts of violence were prohibited, but the final form of the proposed article went further. It also outlawed the mere dissemination of racist ideas, without requiring proof of incitement. An atmosphere of hatred, it was argued by the Polish representative, would inevitably lead to discrimination.

When the draft finally reached the General Assembly, Argentina, Colombia, Ecuador, Panama, and Peru—countries relatively friendly to the United States—proposed deletion of the dissemination-of-ideas language. This amendment was rejected—fifty-four against, twenty-five in favor, and twenty-three abstaining—but the limited consensus on this point indicates the controversial nature of the article.[29] Notably, in other areas of international human rights consensus building, serious ideological controversy dooms a proposal to failure. Language banning anti-Semitism, for example, died a political death because of Arab and Soviet concerns that the charge of anti-Semitism would be used as a political weapon against them.[30] Article 4 is unique in that a clearly controversial proposition survived in the final convention. The survival of Article 4, in spite of the controversy, indicates the overriding strength of the basic idea that promotion of racism is a serious threat to the protection of human rights.

The General Assembly debates on Article 4 focused on free speech. Although the issue was never clearly resolved, it is significant that no country, not even the United States, was willing to abandon the basic premise of Article 4. The article declares that parties "condemn all propaganda . . . based on ideas or theories of superiority . . . or which attempt[s] to justify or promote racial hatred and discrimination in any form."[31] Similarly, the preamble to the convention states explicitly that "any doctrine of. superiority based on racial differentiation is scientifically false, morally condemnable, socially unjust and dangerous, and that there is no justification for racial discrimination."[32] The community of nations has thus made a commitment, with U.S. support, to eliminate racism. It has recognized that racist hate propaganda is illegitimate and is properly subject to control under the international law of human rights. The debate, then, centers around the limits of such control, not around the basic decision to control racism.

The convention, including Article 4, was unanimously adopted by the General Assembly on December 21, 1965.[33] Under UN treaty procedure, it entered into force on January 4, 1969, and gathered an increasing number of state signatures over the years. The United States was an early signatory to the convention, consistent with its significant role in drafting and promoting the convention from the earliest stages. In 1978 President Carter submitted the convention to the Senate for ratification. The Senate has taken no significant steps toward ratification. Signature does not bind the United States to the treaty until the signing is ratified. Under the Vienna Convention on the Law of Treaties, a state's signature does, however, bind it to refrain from defeating the object of the treaty.[34]

The procedure for signature and ratification allows reluctant states to reserve the right to reject antipropaganda laws that would interfere with the right of free speech. Such states apparently felt that the due regard clause of Article 4 was not explicit enough to reserve this right. Some commentators suggest that the United States should not ratify the convention without explicit reservation to Article 4, because the due regard clause is not sufficiently protective of free speech.[35] In signing the convention, the United States made a relatively short reservation, stating:

> The Constitution of the United States contains provisions for the protection of individual rights, such as the right of free speech, and nothing in the Convention shall be deemed to require or to authorize legislation or other action by the United States of America incompatible with the provisions of the Constitution of the United States of America.[36]

This limited reservation indicates the U.S. position of basic support for the convention. Such support is consistent with U.S. ideological commitment to equality and with the need to maintain international prestige. The reservation and the failure to ratify the convention separates the United States from an evolving world standard. As discussed below, this position represents an extreme commitment to the first amendment at the expense of antidiscrimination goals.

The convention is not the only expression of the emerging international view. The need to limit racist hate messages is implicit in basic human rights documents such as the UN Charter and the Universal Declaration of Human Rights. Both documents recognize the primacy of the right to equality and freedom from racism. Other human rights treaties, such as the European Convention for the Protection of Human Rights and Fundamental Freedoms[37] and the American Declaration of the Rights and Duties of Man,[38] also recognize this primacy. The United States is also a party to an international convention on genocide that forbids, *inter alia,* incitement to genocide.[39] Finally, the existing domestic law of several nations—including states that accept the Western notion of freedom of expression—has outlawed certain forms of racist speech.

The United Kingdom, for example, under the Race Relations Act, has criminalized incitement to discrimination and incitement to racial hatred.[40] The act criminalizes the publication or distribution of "threatening, abusive, or insulting" written matter or use of such language in a public place. The United Kingdom standard originally differed from the international standard in that it required proof of intent to incite to hatred. The intent requirement was later dropped.[41] The act is consistent with the international standard in that it recognizes that avoiding the spread of hatred is a legitimate object of the law and that some forms of racist expression are properly criminalized. The legislative history of the act suggests that the drafters were concerned with the spread of racist violence. Imminent violence, however, was not the only object of the act. The act recognized the inevitable connection between the general spread of race hatred and the spread of violence. Although commentators have suggested that the act is ineffective and capable of misuse,[42] the existence of the act supports the growing international movement toward outlawing racist hate propaganda.

Canada has similarly adopted a national statute governing hate propaganda. Sections 318 and 319 of the Canadian Criminal Code[43] outlaw advocacy of genocide, defined as, *inter alia,* an act designed to kill a member of an identifiable group. Also outlawed are communications inciting hatred against any identifiable group where a breach of peace is likely to follow. The law further prohibits the expression of ideas inciting hatred if such expression is tied to a probable threat to order.

The new Canadian Bill of Rights incorporates strong protections for freedom of speech and association.[44] Conflict between the new Bill of Rights and the antihate legislation has not prevented actions to limit hate speech.

Australia and New Zealand also have laws restricting racist speech,[45] leaving the United States alone among the major common law jurisdictions in its complete tolerance of such speech. What the laws of these other countries and the UN convention have in common is that they specify a particularly egregious form of expression for criminalization. All expression concerning differences between races is not banned. The definitive elements are discrimination, connection to violence, and messages of inferiority, hatred, or persecution. Thus the entire spectrum of what could be called racist speech is not prohibited. A belief in intellectual differences between the races, for instance, is not subject to sanctions unless it is coupled with an element of hatred or persecution. What the emerging global standard prohibits is the kind of expression that most interferes with the rights of subordinated-group members to participate equally in society and maintain their basic sense of security and worth as human beings.

The failure of U.S. law to accept this emerging standard reflects a unique first amendment jurisprudence. This jurisprudence is so entrenched in U.S. law that it at first seems irreconcilable with the values given primacy in Article 4, such as the values of equality and full participation. To discuss the significance of this contradiction, it is necessary to consider the U.S. position of tolerance.

U.S. Protection of Racist Hate Propaganda: The Civil Libertarian's Story

Many foreign lawyers, including those from countries close to the United States in ideology, are perplexed by the uniquely American approach of protecting racist hate organizations. American citizens themselves express frustration when they find that the Klan and the Nazis are free to march in public places, with publicly financed police protection. This section will state the U.S. position and attempt to make its strongest case. This is a starting point for exploring the dominant story of racism in American social life and for showing that the U.S. position is neither inevitable nor sound as a matter of democratic theory, constitutional doctrine, or value.

By the U.S. position, I refer to the position that would require reservation to Article 4 and forbearance from other efforts to control racist speech on the ground that restriction of racist hate propaganda and hate organizations is incompatible with the first amendment. As there is no single authoritative assertion of this position, here I address a composite of mainstream first amendment thinking.

Getting a clear statement of the U.S. position is not easy. First amendment doctrine is notably confused, but a reading of the cases reveals the following core ideas. Freedom of expression, the argument goes, is the most fundamental right protected under the Constitution. Democratic, representative government presumes that people are free to think and say whatever they might, even the unthinkable. They can advocate the end of democracy. We risk the chance that they will prevail because to give government the power to control expression is an even greater threat. Power is jealous, and the temptation to stifle legitimate opposition is too great. Thus under our system, there is "no such thing as a false idea."[46] All ideas deserve a public forum, and the way to combat antidemocratic ideas is through counter-expression. When all ideas are voiced freely, we have the greatest chance of obtaining the right results.

We have no way of knowing what the right results are in advance. Ideas that were once accepted as truth we now reject. Because our ideas about what we want as a society are changing and emergent, we cannot say that certain ideas are unacceptable. New ideas often meet opposition, and we have seen new ideas, including major advances in civil rights, eventually become the majority position. We have no basis for distinguishing good from bad ideas, and the only logical choice is to protect all ideas.

If the state feels threatened by certain ideas, it is not without recourse. It can use education and counterspeech to combat those ideas. It can control conduct or action arising from those ideas. Thus although the state cannot outlaw a militaristic political party, it can control the stockpiling of weaponry and punish any acts of violence. Incitement to imminent violence is a related and acceptable point of intervention. Such control is admittedly less effective than direct and preventive repression, but we have made the commitment to a free society, and we will not become unfree even in self-defense. To do otherwise abandons the basic foundation of democracy, rendering nonsensical any claim to necessity. Furthermore, if we accept that ours is a racist society, that is all the more reason to give primacy to the first amendment. The best means to combat racist oppression is the right of protest.

Accepting this extreme commitment to the first amendment is neither easy nor natural. It is a concept one must learn, and it barely survives the hard cases. There is much speech that comes close to action. Conspiratorial speech, inciting speech, fraudulent speech, obscene speech, and defamatory speech are examples of words that seem to emerge from human mouths as more than ideas. Examples might include a merchant's lies about the efficacy of a product, a gang leader's order to murder an enemy, a sexual description broadcast to an audience of children, and threats of physical harm. The U.S. doctrine recognizes a few limited categories of speech that take on qualities beyond expression. These areas are doctrinally distinct, and our commitment to the first amendment value requires the most vigilant scrutiny to avoid suppression of ideas under the guise of controlling conduct.

What the U.S. position means in the area of race is that expressions of the ideas of racial inferiority or racial hatred are protected. Anyone who wants to say that African Americans and Jews are inferior and deserving of persecution is entitled to. However loathsome this idea may be, it is still political speech. The law becomes strong at its edges. If we can hold fast to freedom when it is most difficult to do so, we will avoid making the easy and disastrous mistakes.

The strongest argument against criminalization of racist speech is that it is content-based. It puts the state in the censorship business, with no means of assuring that the censor's hand will go lightly over "good" as opposed to "bad" speech. Critics cite the Canadian experience of words of protest and satire mistakenly challenged using race-hatred laws or the British experience in which censorship of racism is accompanied by censorship of political dissidents. If we outlaw the Ku Klux Klan as an organization repugnant to democratic values, then we can outlaw the Communist party for the same reasons. Admitting one exception will lead to another, and yet another, until those in power are free to stifle opposition in the name of protecting democratic ideals.

A related and less persuasive argument is the "fresh-air" position. This position suggests that the most effective way to control the Klan is to allow it to broadcast its ideas. When people are exposed to the hatred propagated by the Klan, they will reject the Klan and organize against it. Suppressing the Klan will only force it to choose more violent and clandestine means of obtaining its goals.

A corollary to the U.S. position of protection of racist expression is that the government must take certain affirmative steps to preserve that right. The state must make public facilities available on a nondiscriminatory basis to individuals and groups wishing to express their race hatred.[47] It must provide police protection to preserve order and protect speakers who are threatened by counterdemonstrators.[48] Because groups like the Klan typically draw angry opposition when they parade in public streets, these groups have become entitled to publicly financed police escorts. Without this, the right of free speech is meaningless. Angry and intolerant majorities could prevent unpopular minorities from using public facilities, rendering the right of free speech illusory.

The strong first amendment position outlined above represents certain values that are part of the American structure of government and commitment to political and civil rights. The U.S. position may be extreme, but it responds to our history. It recalls the times when our commitment to freedom was tested—the Sedition Act, the McCarthy era, the movement for racial justice, the riots and protests of the Vietnam age. Our commitment to the position has been neither steadfast nor universal. Judges have sometimes failed to understand it, resulting in loose doctrinal ends. The basic principle, however, has survived, and the thrust of the cases and commentary supports first amendment primacy.

The purpose of stating the strongest possible case for the U.S. position is not merely to set the groundwork for an attack. The basic values of freedom of expression, although not provable in any natural law sense, are accepted by the international community. That the American commitment to the ideology of freedom has contributed to social progress and the limitation of repression is a part of our history. The questions presented here are whether the values of the first amendment are in irresolvable conflict with the international movement toward elimination of racist hate propaganda and whether any attempt to move U.S. law toward the international standard is worthwhile.

As a starting point in understanding what is really going on in the law of freedom of expression, it is helpful to note where the edges are. There are several forms of speech that are not entitled to the same protection that existing doctrine would afford racist propaganda.

In the area of commerce and industrial relations, expression is frequently limited. False statements about products, suggestions that prices be fixed, opinions about the value of stock, and proemployer propaganda during union elections are all examples of expressions of ideas that are limited by the law. An instrumental analysis might be that smooth operation of the entities of commerce and the need for a stable setting for the growth of capital have overcome the commitment to civil liberties in these instances. A doctrinal first amendment explanation is that those are examples of hard cases, representing more than the expression of an idea. Some statements are noncommunicative acts, subject to legal restraint. Alternatively, some would argue that many existing exceptions are simply a mistake.

Speech and associational rights are limited in certain professional contexts. Government employees are forbidden to engage in political activity to avoid problems of undue influence. Those charged with the public trust are asked to profess loyalty to the Constitution and limit expression that could undermine their ability to do their job. The class of speakers less favored by the courts has included, dubiously, children and prisoners. These exceptions suggest that internal security and the functioning of government are other policies that override the first amendment in specific cases, to the legitimate discomfort of committed civil libertarians.

The override occurs again in the area of privacy and defamation. Expressing intimate and private facts about a private individual is subject to civil damages, as is the spread of untruths damaging to either public or private figures. First amendment protections are worked into the law of defamation and privacy, but they are not allowed to supersede completely the reputational interest and personal integrity of the victims of certain forms of expression. When courts are called into private disputes about defamatory speech, they are really mediating between competing interests of constitutional dimension: the right of expression, and the implicit right to a measure of personal integrity, peace of mind, and personhood.

Speech infringing on public order is another classic unprotected area. Bomb threats, incitements to riot, "fighting words," and obscene phone calls are a few of the speech-crimes that slip through the first amendment's web of protection. These categories edge close to the category of racist speech. Under existing law, insults of such dimension that they bring men— this is a male-centered standard—to blows are subject to a first amendment exception. The problem is that racist speech is so common that it is seen as part of the ordinary jostling and conflict people are expected to tolerate, rather than as fighting words. Another problem is that the effect of de- humanizing racist language on the target is often flight rather than fight. Targets choose to avoid racist encounters whenever possible, internalizing the harm rather than escalating the conflict. Lack of a fight and admirable self-restraint then defines the words as nonactionable.

Although it is sometimes suggested that the first amendment is absolute, even strong civil libertarians are likely to admit that the absolutist view is unworkable. The law professor Frederick Schauer has argued that absolute protection of expression would render unconstitutional "all of contract law, most of antitrust law, and much of criminal law."[49] The need to distinguish protected from unprotected speech is inevitable.

If there are important competing interests represented in the inter- national position on elimination of racist hate messages, if these interests are only met by limiting speech, and if the speech represented in racist hate propaganda is not the kind of speech most needful of protection, then it may be possible to remain true to the first amendment without protecting racist hate propaganda. In the following section I suggest that an explicit and narrow definition of racist hate messages will allow restriction consistent with first amendment values.

Narrow Application and Protection of First Amendment Values

This chapter attempts to recognize and accommodate the civil libertarian position. The victim's perspective requires respect for the idea of rights, for it is those on the bottom who are most hurt by the absence of rights, and it is those on the bottom who have sustained the struggle for rights in U.S. history. The image of book burnings should unnerve us and remind us to argue long and hard before selecting a class of speech to exclude from the public domain. I am uncomfortable in making the suggestions in this section when others fall too easily into agreement.

A definition of actionable racist speech must be narrow in order to respect first amendment values. I believe racist speech is best treated as a sui generis category, presenting an idea so historically untenable, so dangerous, and so tied to perpetuation of violence and degradation of the very classes of human beings who are least equipped to respond that it is properly treated as outside the realm of protected discourse. The courts in the *Skokie* case[50] expressed doubt that principles were available to single out racist speech for public limitation. Here I attempt to construct a doctrinal and evidentiary world in which we might begin to draw the lines the *Skokie* courts could not imagine.

The alternative to recognizing racist speech as qualitatively different because of its content is to continue to stretch existing first amendment exceptions, such as the "fighting words" doctrine and the "content/conduct" distinction. This stretching ultimately weakens the first amendment fabric, creating neutral holes that remove protection for many forms of speech. Setting aside the worst forms of racist speech for special treatment is a non-neutral, value-laden approach that will better preserve free speech.

To distinguish the worst, paradigm example of racist hate messages from other forms of racist and nonracist speech, I offer three identifying characteristics:

1. The message is of racial inferiority
2. The message is directed against a historically oppressed group
3. The message is persecutory, hateful, and degrading

Making each element a prerequisite to prosecution prevents opening of the dreaded floodgates of censorship.

The first element is the primary identifier of racist speech: Racist speech proclaims racial inferiority and denies the personhood of target-group members. All members of the target group are at once considered alike and inferior.

The second element attempts to further define racism by recognizing the connection of racism to power and subordination. Racism is more than race hatred or prejudice. It is the structural subordination of a group based on an idea of racial inferiority. Racist speech is particularly harmful because it is a mechanism of subordination, reinforcing a historical vertical relationship.

The final element is related to the "fighting words" idea. The language used in the worst form of racist speech is language that is, and is intended as, persecutory, hateful, and degrading.

The following section applies these three elements to hypothetical cases. Using these elements narrows the field of interference with speech. Under these narrowing elements, arguing that particular groups are genetically superior in a context free of hatefulness and without the endorsement of persecution is permissible. Satire and stereotyping that avoids persecutory language remains protected. Hateful verbal attacks upon dominant-group members by victims is permissible. These kinds of speech are offensive, but they are, in respect of first amendment principles, best subjected to the marketplace of ideas. This is not to suggest that we remain silent in the face of offensive speech of this type. Rather, the range of private remedies—

including counterspeech, social approbation, boycott, and persuasion—should apply.

If the most egregious, paradigmatic racial hate messages are not properly left to private remedy, it is important to explain why. One way to explain this is to consider the difference between racist hate messages and Marxist speech. Marxist speech is the kind of unpopular political expression the first amendment is intended to protect. Marxist speech is, according to a once-prevalent view, the advocacy of overthrow of existing governments, inevitably leading to dictatorships and persecution of dissidents and capitalists. It is thus, it was argued, dangerous speech, properly censored. The legacy of this view was McCarthyism and the shattered lives of hundreds of decent citizens.

How can one argue for censorship of racist hate messages without encouraging a revival of McCarthyism? There is an important difference that comes from human experience, our only source of collective knowledge. We know, from our collective historical knowledge, that slavery was wrong. We know white minority rule in South Africa is wrong. This knowledge is reflected in the universal acceptance of the wrongness of the doctrine of racial supremacy. There is no nation left on this planet that submits as its national self-expression the view that Hitler was right. South Africa is alone in its official policy of apartheid, and even South Africa, in making its case to the world community, is careful to avoid an explicit ideology of racial supremacy, preferring instead the rhetoric of one step at a time. At the universities, at the centers of knowledge of the international community, the doctrines of racial supremacy and racial hatred are again uniformly rejected. At the United Nations the same is true. We have fought wars and spilled blood to establish the universal acceptance of this principle. The universality of the principle, in a world bereft of agreement on many things, is a mark of collective human progress. The victim's perspective, one mindful of the lessons of history, thus accepts racist speech as sui generis and universally condemned.

Marxist speech, however, is not universally condemned. Marxism presents a philosophy for political organization, distribution of wealth and power, ordering of values, and promotion of social change. By its very content it is political speech going to the core of ongoing political debate. It is impossible to achieve world consensus either for or against this political view. Marxists teach in universities. Although Marxist ideas are rejected and abhorred by many, Marxist thought, like liberal thought, neoconservative economic theory, and other conflicting structures for understanding life and politics, is part of the ongoing efforts of human beings to understand their world and improve life in it.

What is argued here, then, is that we accept certain principles as the shared historical legacy of the world community. Racial supremacy is one of the ideas we have collectively and internationally considered and rejected. As an idea connected to continuing racism and degradation of minority groups, it causes real harm to its victims. We are not safe when these violent words are among us.

Treating racist speech as sui generis and universally condemned on the basis of its content and the harmful effect of its content is precisely the censorship that civil libertarians fear. I would argue, however, that explicit content-based rejection of narrowly defined racist speech is more protective of civil liberties than the competing-interests tests or the likely-to-incite-violence tests that can spill over to censor forms of political speech.

Looking to the emerging critical race theory, I derive basic principles: the need to fight racism at all levels, the value of explicit formal rules, and a fear of tyranny. These principles suggest the wisdom of legal intervention with only a narrowly defined class of racist hate propaganda.

A range of legal interventions, including the use of tort law and criminal law principles, is appropriate to combat racist hate propaganda. Although the value of free speech can guide the choice of procedure—including evidentiary rules and burdens of persuasion—it should not completely remove recourse to the institution of law to combat racist speech. Racism as an acquired set of behaviors can be disacquired, and law is the means by which the state typically provides incentives for changes in behavior.

Hard Cases

In order to get beyond racism, we must first take account of race. There is no other way.
—Harry Blackmun[51]

Of course I emphasize different things, Doctor, because history has treated my people differently from yours.
—Richard Delgado[52]

In this section I consider stories at the edge, a tentative discussion of problem cases that may arise under the definition of actionable racist speech discussed here. The connecting thread in these examples is the need for clarity about the historical context in which racist speech arises and attention to the degree of harm experienced by targets of different kinds of racist speech.

A Case of the Angry Nationalist

Expressions of hatred, revulsion, and anger directed against members of historically dominant groups by subordinated-group members are not criminalized by the definition of racist hate messages used here. Malcolm X's "white devil" statements—which he later retracted—are an example. Some would find this troublesome, arguing that any attack on any person's ethnicity is harmful. In the case of the white devil, there is harm and hurt, but it is of a different degree. Because the attack is not tied to the perpetuation of racist vertical relationships, it is not the paradigm worst example of hate propaganda. The dominant-group member hurt by conflict with the angry nationalist is more likely to have access to a safe harbor of exclusive dominant-group interactions. Retreat and reaffirmation of personhood are more easily attained for members of groups not historically subjugated.

Although white-hating nationalist expressions are condemnable both politically and personally, I would interpret an angry, hateful poem by a person from a historically subjugated group as a victim's struggle for self-identity in response to racism. It is not tied to the structural domination of another group. Part of the special harm of racist speech is that it works in concert with other racist tools to keep victim groups in an inferior position. Should history change course, placing former victim groups in a dominant or equalized position, the newly equalized group will lose the special protection suggested here for expression of nationalist anger.

Critics of this proposal ask how one knows who is oppressed and who is not. Poor whites, ethnic whites, wealthy ethnics—the confusing examples and barriers to classification abound. The larger question is how anyone knows anything in life or in law. To conceptualize a condition called subordination is a legitimate alternative to denying that such a condition exists. In law we conceptualize. We take on mammoth tasks of discovery and knowing. We can determine when subordination exists by looking at social indicators: Wealth, mobility, comfort, health, and survival—or the absence of these—tend to mark the rise to the top and the fall to the depths. The rise and fall of group status is relevant even when an individual is a counterexample, because when the group is subordinated, even the lucky counterexample feels the downward tug. Luck is not the same as privilege.

In some cases, a group's social well-being may improve even as its victimization continues. Asians who experience economic success are often underemployed relative to their talents. Jews who attain equality in employment still experience anti-Semitic vilification, harassment, and exclusion. Catholics are relatively free from discrimination in some communities and subject to vile bigotry in others. Evidence of the relative subjugation of various groups is available to fact finders.

In the same way that lawyers marshal evidence in an adversarial setting to find facts in other areas of law, we can learn to know the facts about subordination and to determine when hate speech is used as an instrument of that subordination.

First Variation: Anti-Semitism and Racism Within Subordinated Communities

What of hateful racist and anti-Semitic speech by people within subordinated communities? The phenomenon of one subordinated group inflicting racist speech upon another subordinated group is a persistent and touchy problem. Similarly, members of a subordinated group sometimes direct racist language at their own group. The victim's privilege becomes problematic when it is used by one subordinated person to lash out at another. I argue here for tolerance of hateful speech that comes from an experience of oppression, but when that speech is used to attack a subordinated-group member, using language of persecution and adopting a rhetoric of racial inferiority, I am inclined to prohibit such speech.

History and context are important in this case because the custom in a particular subordinated community may tolerate racial insults as a form of wordplay. Where this is the case, community members tend to have a clear sense of what is racially degrading and what is not. The appropriate standard in determining whether language is persecutory, hateful, and degrading is the recipient's community standard. We should beware lest by misunderstanding linguistic and cultural norms we further entrench structures of subordination.

Second Variation: Zionism

I reject the sweeping charge that Zionism is racism and argue instead for a highly contextualized consideration of Zionist speech. To the extent that any racial hostility expressed within a Zionist context is a reaction to historical persecution, it is protected under the doctrinal scheme suggested in this chapter. Should Zionists ever lose this historically based privilege? If Zionist speakers are white, do hateful, race-bound expressions of theirs necessarily reinforce historical conditions of white dominance over brown and black people? The analysis must turn on the particular context. If a Zionist's expression of anger includes a statement of generic white supremacy and persecution, the speaker chooses to ally with a larger, historically dominant group, and the privilege should not apply. On the other hand, angry, survivalist expression, arising out of the Jewish experience of persecution and without resort to the rhetoric of generic white supremacy, is protected under the contextualized approach. Again, it is important to add that the various subordinated communities are best equipped to analyze and condemn hate speech arising within their midst.

The Case of the Dead-Wrong Social Scientist

Another difficult case is that of the social scientist who makes a case for racial inferiority in an academic setting based on what is presented as scientific evidence. Various theories of genetic predisposition to violence, cultural lag, and a correlation between race and intelligence fall into this category. Critics note that these pseudoscientific theories are racist and ignorant.[53] This raises two separate questions. First, should such views receive an audience and a forum in an academic setting? Second, should we criminalize expressions of such views?

As to the first question, the answer may well be no. Not all views deserve the dignity of an academic forum. Poorly documented, racially biased work does not meet the professional standards required of academic writing. If a writer manages to come up with a theory of racial inferiority supported by evidence acceptable within the relevant discipline, that theory may deserve a forum. Under the principle of academic freedom, ignorant views need not be heard, but unpopular, academically tenable views should be.

As to the second question, outlawing this type of speech might be inappropriate. Assuming the dead-wrong social science theory of inferiority is free of any message of hatred and persecution, the ordinary, private solution is sufficient: Attack such theories with open public debate and with denial of a forum if the work is unsound in its documentation.

The Case of Wordless Speech: Symbols and Regalia, Text and Context

There are certain symbols and regalia that in the context of history carry a clear message of racial supremacy, hatred, persecution, and degradation of certain groups. The swastika, the Klan robes, the burning cross are examples of signs that—like all signs—have no meaning on their own, but convey a powerful message to both the user and the recipient of the sign in context.

Here we must look to the history of these signs to understand what they mean. If the historical message, known to both victim and perpetrator, is racist persecution and violence, then the sign is properly treated as actionable racist speech.

The Cold Version of the Classic Forms of Anti-Semitism

Anti-Semitic literature is one of the most highly developed and despicable forms of hate propaganda. A significant problem with the test proposed here is that it may, at first blush, seem too narrow to cover some chillingly sterile brands of anti-Semitic literature. The monetary conspiracy theories, the tales of mysterious cartels, the revisionist histories distributed by anti-Semitic hate groups are sometimes cunningly devoid of explicit hate language. Here is another story:

One recent summer, after giving a talk advocating restriction of hate speech, I was dutifully catching up on reading academic junk mail—newsletters, book announcements, requests for contributions. I picked up a leaflet, professionally printed and attributed to an academic institution, and began reading what looked like a mildly interesting historical essay. It was only after several paragraphs that I realized I was reading a holocaust hoax tract. My heart started racing as soon as I realized what a horrible thing I held in my hand. I felt fear and revulsion that I was targeted to receive this mail and that it was written in such a way that I didn't immediately recognize it for what it was. I fished in the

*rubbish can for the envelope and found it had no return address—that should
have been the tip-off. The out-of-state postmark gave me some relief. At least the
writers were not in my immediate neighborhood. The fear, however, remains,
and I am more cautious about where and to whom I will speak on this topic that
brings hate to my desk.*

I am inclined to criminalize the cold-blooded version of anti-Semitic literature. Given the historical record, this "cold" version is just as hateful, for all
its tone of distorted rationality, as the "hot" name-calling versions. To call
the Holocaust a myth is to defame the dead, as Elie Wiesel has so eloquently
put it.[54] It is a deep harm to the living. In a range of different contexts, the
common law has recognized the likelihood of emotional harm to the living
from careless treatment of the dead.

The element of hatred and degradation is present in the monetary
conspiracy theory and holocaust hoax literature. Like the swastika, these
texts take their hateful meaning from their historical context and connection
to violence. To anyone who knows that context, they cause legitimate
distress.

Collections, Museums, Neutral Reportage, Humor, and Literary Realism

> *YES! Send me* The SS, *to examine for 10 days free, as my introduction to* The Third
> Reich.
> —Advertisement for Time-Life Books[55]

There are instances in which hate propaganda is deliberately spread by
persons who are not themselves hate mongers. There are groups that
preserve and disseminate hate propaganda for the purpose of educating the
public about the evils of racism and anti-Semitism. There are groups and
individuals who collect racist memorabilia for reasons of collectability, some
also claiming an educative function and others out of a fondness for the
ephemera of evil. There are news reporters who repeat racist speech in
reporting the news of its utterance, law professors who repeat racist words
in hypotheticals for class discussion of the first amendment. In these cases
the hate message is spread for purposes other than persecution. The hateful
message is once removed from direct transmission by a buffer zone of a
nonpersecuting presenter.

When I viewed an Anti-Defamation League display of Nazi propaganda, I
felt a familiar, queasy revulsion—the same feeling I got when I viewed dusty
spoils of war, emblazoned with swastikas, at the veterans' halls I visited with
my father as a child. What I did not feel was the heart-racing fear engendered
by hate propaganda from anonymous senders. Knowing the intent of the
Anti-Defamation League made the presentation less intrusive. Knowing that

the league is in constant dialogue with victim-group members, carefully considering the possible harms of neutral presentations of hate propaganda, was a significant comfort.

The growing passion for collecting racist memorabilia is more troublesome. Not all collectors are involved in careful debate, weighing the harm of insult against the value of historic preservation. State intervention might be appropriate where collectors' displays cause gratuitous harm to viewers. The key to differentiating between the Anti-Defamation League display and a hypothetical Gestapo Collector's Club display of lovingly polished storm trooper paraphernalia is the victim's story. Rather than looking to the neutral, objective, unknowing, and ahistorical reasonable person, we should look to the victim-group members to tell us whether there is real harm to real people.

Another area of seemingly less egregious speech is humor. Consider this comment by an American judge: "Do you know how to make an [ethnic group] omelette? Well, first you have to go out and steal three eggs."[56] Not only are these jokes unfunny, they are also cruel and hurtful in much the same way that racist epithets are. That they are said with a smile and often in a social or performance setting that may be a somewhat more appropriate venue for insult changes their character somewhat. It is a venue in which private sanction has some opportunity for success. The comedian Richard Pryor, for example, stated publicly that he was persuaded to discontinue comedic use of a racial epithet in his performances.

Similarly, in considering the use of racist slurs in the interests of realism in books, films, and theater, the experience of victim-group members is a guide. The writer-director Spike Lee's film *Do the Right Thing*[57] contains a rapid-fire sequence of racial epithets spoken by characters from different racial groups in a Brooklyn neighborhood. The hyperrealism of the sequence offers an incisive antiracist critique of racist speech. Similarly, Mark Twain, known as a great American writer and antiracist, used racist dialogue to portray a racist land. The problem for some African-American parents is that their young children may suffer harm from further exposure to racist language, particularly in a white-majority setting. Students of color frequently report feeling assaulted in classrooms where racist epithets are used casually, and even gleefully, by classmates who claim they are only reporting the racist words of others.

The failure of school integration and the underrepresentation of African Americans in positions of authority in the schools increases the danger that Twain's realism will, in some schools, cause the kind of harm Twain himself would have abhorred. We need safe harbors before we begin rocking boats.

Consider this story:

A white teacher in Gould, Arkansas, resigned in tears after parental protests over her statement to boisterous school children, "I think you're trying to make me think you're a bunch of poor, dumb n———rs, and I don't think that." Seats on the school board and other positions of authority in that town of 60 percent African-American residency were occupied by African Americans. Students signed petitions urging the school board to reconsider its actions against the teacher and to give her a second chance. The teacher was reinstated, expressing sincere regret for her error and her thanks to the students for a second chance. A picture of the smiling white teacher embracing an African-American student leader accompanies the news item.[58]

Would that all incidents of hate speech had that ending: victims empowered, consciousness raised, community restored, harm kept at bay. Unfortunately for most of us, the conditions necessary for the result achieved in that small Arkansas town are not the conditions we live under. The harm of racist speech slices deeper the farther away we are from such a life.

The Special Case of Universities

A marked rise of racial harassment, hate speech, and racially motivated violence marks the beginning of the 1990s. The epidemic of racist incidents on university campuses is a disturbing example of this. The application of the first amendment to racist speech, once discussed hypothetically in law schools, is now debated in classrooms where hate messages have actually appeared. The current judicial opinions tangling with hate speech and the first amendment often come from the universities.

The university case raises unique concerns. Universities are special places, charged with pedagogy and duty bound to a constituency with special vulnerabilities. Many of the new adults who come to live and study at the major universities are away from home for the first time and at a vulnerable stage of psychological development. The typical university student is emotionally vulnerable for several reasons. College is a time of emancipation from a preexisting home or community, of development of identity, of dependence-independence conflict, of major decisionmaking, and of formulation of future plans. The move to college often involves geographic relocation—a major life-stress event—and the forging of new peer ties to replace old ones. All of these stresses and changes render the college years critical in development of one's outlook on life. College students experiment with different passions, identities, and risks. A negative environmental response during this period of experimentation could mar for life an individual's ability to remain open, creative, and risk taking.[59] Students are particularly dependent on the university for community, for intellectual development, and for self-definition. Official tolerance of racist speech in this setting is more harmful than generalized tolerance in the community at large. It is harmful to student perpetrators in that it is a lesson in getting away with it that will have lifelong repercussions. It is harmful to targets, who perceive the university as taking sides through inaction and who are left to their own resources in coping with the damage wrought. Finally, it is a harm to the goals of inclusion, education, development of knowledge, and ethics that universities exist and stand for. Lessons of cynicism and hate replace lessons in critical thought and inquiry.

The campus free speech issues of the Vietnam era and those evoked by the antiapartheid movement pit students against university administrators, multinational corporations, the U.S. military, and established governments. In the context of that kind of power imbalance, the free speech rights of students deserve particular deference. Unfortunately, as we know from our memory of four dead in Ohio, that deference is not always forthcoming.

Racist speech on campus occurs in a vastly different power context. Campus racism targets vulnerable students and faculty. Students of color often come to the university at risk academically, socially, and psychologically. Faculty of color—if they exist at all—are typically untenured, overburdened, and isolated.[60] The marginalized position of faculty of color further marginalizes students of color.

There is legal precedent for considering the status of the target in measuring the amount of freedom verbal attackers enjoy. In the law of defamation, private figures can more easily obtain damages for harm to their reputation than can public figures. This is based on the greater ability of public figures to launch an effective rebuttal and on their voluntary choice to enter the public eye. An additional implicit justification is that wealth, power, and fame provide ego support that helps one weather verbal abuse. If nothing else, the defamed movie star can retreat to Malibu.

The student, like the private figure, has fewer avenues of retreat. Living on or near campus, studying in the library, and interacting with fellow students are integral parts of university life. When racist propaganda appears on campus, target-group students experience debilitated access to the full university experience. This is so even when hate propaganda is directed at groups rather than at individuals.

Students are analogous to the captive audience that is afforded special first amendment consideration in other contexts. Similarly, students who support universities through tuition and who are encouraged to think of the university as their home are involuntarily forced into a position of complicity with racism when their campus is offered to hate groups as a forum.

A related and literally captive group deserves mention here. The majority of prison inmates in many communities are people of color. Prisons are also fertile grounds for spreading racist hate speech. Courts have protected the rights of hate groups in prisons. The physical vulnerability and inability to escape that characterize prison life make restriction of hate speech in prisons more important than in the population at large.

Summary: Expanded Relevance and the Hard Cases

Terse epithets come down to our generation weighted with hatreds accumulated through centuries of bloodshed.

—Justice Robert H. Jackson[61]

If we want to be whole, we must recall the past, those parts which we want to remember, those parts which we want to forget.

—Barbara Christian[62]

The cases discussed above are an effort to construct the conversation we might have if we take on the task of delineating and penalizing the most harmful class of racist speech. It is not an impossible conversation. It is a different one, in that it suggests a highly contextualized analysis and a range of relevant evidence quite at odds with that found in typical legal inquiry. This evidence encompasses the particularity of a victim's time and place as well as the experience of a victim's group over the course of time and space. It recognizes that the experience of racism, of persecution for membership in a group, makes the group's consciousness the victim's consciousness, all of which is relevant in assessing the harm of racist speech. It makes relevant, then, knowledge as old as the Torah and as new as the back page of this morning's newspaper. It makes relevant, too, what has happened to you, to me, to an acquaintance, to a friend of a friend, to a person whom we have never met but who is tied to us as a survivor of the same hate.

This deep historical consciousness lifts us out of the neutrality trap, that trap under which many states have passed antimask statutes in a barely disguised effort to limit Ku Klux Klan activities.[63] These statutes purportedly cover the wearing of masks in general, with no specific mention of the intent to control the Klan. Neutral reasons, such as the need to prevent pickpockets from moving unidentified through crowds or the need to unmask burglars and bank robbers are proffered for such statutes. The result of forgetting—or pretending to forget—the real reason for antimask legislation is farcical. Masks are used in protest against terrorist regimes for reasons of both symbolism and personal safety. Iranian students wearing masks and opposing human rights violations by the Shah of Iran, for example, were prosecuted under a California antimask statute.

I call here for an end of such unknowing. We know why state legislatures—those quirkily populist institutions—have passed antimask statutes. It is more honest, and less cynically manipulative of legal doctrine, to legislate openly against the worst forms of racist speech, allowing ourselves to know what we know.

The Unintended Story: The Meaning of Legal Protection of Racist Hate Messages

The legal response to racist propaganda provides an interesting context for examination of the relation between law and racism. Legal protection of racism is seen in these doctrinal elements:

1. The limits of doctrinal imagination in creating first amendment exceptions for racist hate speech
2. The refusal to recognize the competing values of liberty and equality at stake in the case of hate speech
3. The refusal to view the protection of racist speech as a form of state action

The limits of the lawmaking imagination of judges, legislators, and other legal insiders who have considered proposals to outlaw hate propaganda are symptomatic of the position of privilege from which legal doctrine develops. Legal insiders cannot imagine a life disabled in a significant way by hate propaganda.

This limited imagination has not affected lawmakers faced with other forms of offensive speech. The law of defamation and privacy recognizes that certain forms of expression are qualitatively different from the kind of speech deserving absolute protection. The legal imagination is able to contemplate what it feels like to hear lies spread about one's professional competency or to have one's likeness used for commercial gain without consent. American law has even, at times, provided a tort remedy for white plaintiffs who are "insulted" by "imputation of association with persons of a race against which there is prejudice."[64] When the legal mind understands that reputational interests, which are analogized to the preferred interest in property, must be balanced against first amendment interests, it recognizes the concrete reality of what happens to people who are defamed. Their lives are changed. Their standing in the community, their opportunities, their self-worth, their free enjoyment of life are limited. Their political capital—their ability to speak and be heard—is diminished. To see this, and yet to fail to see that the very same things happen to the victims of racist speech, is selective vision.

The selective consideration of one victim's story and not another's results in unequal application of the law. Unlike the victims of defamation and other torts, the victims of racist speech are not representative of the population at large. In making typical legal concessions to the first amendment, we burden a range of victims. In the case of flag burning, we force flag lovers of all races and class positions to tolerate flag desecration as part of the price of freedom. In contrast, when victims of racist speech are left to assuage their own wounds, we burden a limited class: the traditional victims of discrimination.

This class already experiences diminished access to private remedies such as effective counterspeech, and this diminished access is exacerbated by hate messages. As the feminist scholar Catharine MacKinnon notes, debasing speech discredits targets, further reducing their ability to have their speech taken seriously.[65] The application of absolutist free speech principles to hate speech, then, is a choice to burden one group with a disproportionate share of the costs of speech promotion. Tolerance of hate speech thus creates superregressivity—those least able to pay are the only ones taxed for this tolerance. The principle of equality is violated by such allocation. The more progressive principle of rectification or reparation—the obligation to repair effects of historical wrongs—is even more grossly violated.

The failure to hear the victim's story results in an inability to give weight to competing values of constitutional dimension. The competing values recognized under international law are equality, liberty, and personality. Each person under that scheme is entitled to basic dignity, to nondiscrimination, and to the freedom to participate fully in society. If there is any central principle to the Bill of Rights, surely that is it. When white supremacist organizations with histories of violence have an active, protected presence in a community, that principle is sacrificed. All of our democratic institutions are tainted as a consequence. As Delgado notes in Chapter 4, the underlying first amendment values of self-fulfillment, knowledge, participation, and stable community recognized by first amendment theorists are sacrificed when hate speech is protected. The constitutional commitment to equality and the promise to abolish the badges and incidents of slavery are emptied of meaning when target-group members must alter their behavior, change their choice of neighborhood, leave their jobs, and warn their children off the streets because of hate group activity. When the presence of the Klan deters employers from hiring target-group members, prevents citizens from socializing freely, and keeps parents from sending their children to integrated schools, the goal of nondiscrimination is moved farther away from present realities. When hate propaganda spreads attitudes of racism and desensitizes potential abusers to the wrongness of violence, other more obvious goals of safety and order are sacrificed.

The third doctrinal pillar supporting racist speech is the refusal to recognize that tolerance and protection of hate group activity by the government is a form of state action. Hate groups have operated openly in prisons, in the military, in law enforcement, and in other government institutions. To allow an organization known for violence, persecution, race hatred, and commitment to racial supremacy to exist openly and to provide police protection and access to public facilities, streets, and college campuses for such a group means that the state is promoting racist speech. But for such support, hate groups would decline in efficacy. The chilling sight of avowed racists in threatening regalia marching through our neighborhoods with full police protection is a statement of state authorization. The Klan marches because marching promotes the Klan and because of the terrorizing and inciting effect of its public displays. Open display conveys legitimacy. The government advances this effect when it protects these marches. In addition, the failure to provide a legal response limiting hate propaganda elevates the liberty interests of racists over the liberty interests of their targets. A member of the Georgia Bureau of Investigation, for example, once suggested to whites targeted for hate speech because of their association with African Americans that they should avoid being seen in cars with African Americans and cease inviting African Americans to their homes.[66]

The effect of racist propaganda is to devalue the individual and to treat masses of people in a degraded way with no measure of individual merit. This is precisely what civil libertarians oppose when the state acts. Because racist speech is seen as private, the connection to loss of liberty is not made. State silence, however, is public action where the strength of the new racist groups derives from their offering legitimation and justification for otherwise socially unacceptable emotions of hate, fear, and aggression. The need for a formal group, for a patriotic cause, and for an elevation of the doubting self are part of the traditional attraction of groups like the Klan. Government protection of the right of the Klan to exist publicly and to spread a racist message promotes the role of the Klan as a legitimizer of racism.

Further, the law's failure to provide recourse to persons who are demeaned by the hate messages is an effective second injury to that person. The second injury is the pain of knowing that the government provides no remedy and offers no recognition of the dehumanizing experience that victims of hate propaganda are subjected to. The government's denial of personhood through its denial of legal recourse may be even more painful than the initial act of hatred. One can dismiss the hate group as an organization of marginal people, but the state is the official embodiment of the society we live in.

The legal realists and their progeny recognize that law formation is largely a matter of value.[67] There are no inevitable results; there is no controlling logic or doctrine that can make the hard choices for us. Reversion to discredited doctrinal absolutism carries a strong implication that racist activities are supported, albeit unintentionally, by the law. In a society that expresses its moral judgments through the law, and in which the rule of law and the use of law are characteristic responses to many social phenomena, this absence of laws against racist speech is telling.

We can defy the proposition that racism is part of law by opening our eyes to the reality of racism and making the decision to outlaw hate groups. We can draw from the international standard and acknowledge the competing interests at stake, adapting existing law and creating new law to limit hate group activities. It is not necessary to abandon first amendment values in order to do this. The analytical dexterity of legal thinkers offers many options for reconciling the U.S. position with the international goal of elimination of all forms of racial discrimination.

This chapter suggests that the stories of those who have experienced racism are of special value in defeating racism. It further suggests that we can, and have, chosen as a primary value freedom from racial oppression. Finally, in doing the awkward work of constructing doctrine, this chapter suggests a belief in the possibility and the necessity of creating a legal response to racist speech—not because it isn't really speech, not because it falls within a hoped-for neutral exception, but because it is wrong.

There is in every constitutional doctrine we devise the danger of misuse. For fear of falling, we are warned against taking a first step. Frozen at the first amendment bulkhead, we watch the rising tide of racial hatred wash over our schools and workplaces. Students victimized by racist speech turn to university administrators for redress and are told that the first amendment forecloses institutional action. We owe those students a more thoughtful analysis than absolutism. At the least, before we abandon the task of devising a legal response to racist speech, we should consider concretely the options available to us. The legal imagination is a fruitful one. That is the one hopeful message of the postmodern critique of law. Nothing inherent in law ties our hands, and lawyers through the ages have displayed abundant skills of invention.

Conclusion

Critical race theory uses the experience of subordination to offer a phenomenology of race and law. The victims' experience reminds us that the harm of racist hate messages is a real harm to real people. When the legal system offers no redress for that real harm, it perpetuates racism.

This chapter attempts to begin a conversation about the first amendment that acknowledges both the civil libertarian's fear of tyranny and the victims' experience of loss of liberty in a society that tolerates racist speech. It suggests criminalization of a narrow, explicitly defined class of racist hate speech to provide public redress for the most serious harm, leaving many forms of racist speech to private remedies. Some may feel that this proposal does not go far enough, leaving much hurtful speech to the uneven control of the marketplace of ideas. Others will cringe at what they perceive as a call for censorship. This is not an easy legal or moral puzzle, but it is precisely in these places where we feel conflicting tugs at heart and mind that we have the most work to do and the most knowledge to gain.

Ours is a law-bound culture. If law is where racism is, then law is where we must confront it. The doctrinal reconstruction presented here is tentative and subject to change as our struggle around this issue continues. However we choose to respond to racist speech, let us present a competing ideology, one that has existed in tension with racism since the birth of our nation: There is inherent worth in each human being, and each is entitled to a life of dignity.

3

If He Hollers Let Him Go: Regulating Racist Speech on Campus

Charles R. Lawrence III

Racist incidents occur at the University of Michigan, University of Massachusetts-Amherst, University of Wisconsin, University of New Mexico, Columbia University, Wellesley College, Duke University, and University of California-Los Angeles. (*Ms.* magazine, October 1987)

The campus ought to be the last place to legislate tampering with the edges of first amendment protections.

University of Michigan:
"Greek Rites of Exclusion": Racist leaflets distributed in dorms; white students paint themselves black and place rings in their noses at "jungle parties." (*The Nation*, July 1987)

Silencing a few creeps is no victory if the price is an abrogation of free speech. Remember censorship is an ugly word too.

Northwest Missouri State University:
White Supremacists distribute flyers stating: "The Knights of the Ku Klux Klan are Watching You." (Klanwatch Intelligence Report No. 42, February 1988 [*Klanwatch*])

Kansas University:
KKK members speak. (*Klanwatch*)

Temple University:
White Student Union formed. (*Klanwatch*)

The title of this chapter was inspired by the novel by Chester Himes, *If He Hollers Let Him Go* (1945).

Stanford University:
Aryan Resistance literature distributed. (*Klanwatch*)

Stockton State College (New Jersey):
Invisible Empire literature distributed. (*Klanwatch*)

Memphis State University:
Bomb threats at Jewish Student Union. (*Klanwatch*)

Arizona State University:
Shot fired at Hillel Foundation building. (*Klanwatch*)

The harm that censors allege will result unless speech is forbidden rarely occurs.

Dartmouth College:
Black professor called "a cross between a welfare queen and a bathroom attendant" and the *Dartmouth Review* purported to quote a Black student, "Dese boys be sayin' that we be comin' here to Dartmut an' not takin' the classics." (*The Nation*, February 27, 1989)

Yes, speech is sometimes painful. Sometimes it is abusive. That is one of the prices of a free society.

Purdue University:
Counselor finds "Death Nigger" scratched on her door. (*The Nation*, February 27, 1989)

More speech, not less, is the proper cure for offensive speech.

Smith College:
African student finds message slipped under her door that reads, "African Nigger do you want some bananas? Go back to the Jungle." (*New York Times*, October 19, 1988)

Speech cannot be banned simply because it is offensive.

University of Michigan:
Campus radio station broadcasts a call from a student who "joked": "Who are the most famous black women in history? Aunt Jemima and Mother Fucker." (*The Nation*, February 27, 1989)

Those who don't like what they are hearing or seeing should try to change the atmosphere through education. That is what they will have to do in the real world after they graduate.

University of Michigan:
A student walks into class and sees this written on the blackboard: "A mind is a terrible thing to waste—especially on a nigger." (*Chicago Tribune*, April 23, 1989)

People of color, women, and gays and lesbians owe their vibrant political movements in large measure to their freedom to communicate. If speech can be banned because it offends someone, how long will it be before the messages of these groups are themselves found offensive?

Stanford University:
"President Donald Kennedy refused yesterday to consider amnesty for students who took over his office last week. . . . Kennedy insisted that the probe of violations of the Stanford behavior code go forward. The students [who were demanding more minority faculty and ethnic studies reforms] consider the prospect of disciplinary action unfair in view of Stanford's decision earlier this year not to punish two white students who defaced a poster of 19th century composer Ludwig von Beethoven to portray a stereotypical black face, then tacked it up in a predominantly black dormitory. The two incidents differ sharply, Kennedy said. The poster was admittedly racially offensive. But its defacement probably was protected by constitutional freedoms. However, the office takeover was clearly a violation of Stanford's policy against campus disruption." (*San Francisco Chronicle*, May 25, 1989)

Now it's the left that is trying to restrict free speech. Though the political labels have shifted, the rationale is the same: Our adversaries are dangerous and therefore should not be allowed to speak.

In recent years, university campuses have seen a resurgence of racial violence and a corresponding rise in the incidence of verbal and symbolic assault and harassment to which blacks and other traditionally subjugated groups are subjected. The events listed above were gathered from newspaper and magazine reports of racist incidents on campuses. The accompanying italicized statements criticizing proposals to regulate racism on campus were garnered from conversations, debates, and panel discussions at which I was present. Some were recorded verbatim and are exact quotes; others paraphrase the sentiment expressed. I have heard some version of each of these arguments many times over. These incidents are but a small sampling of the hate speech to which minorities are subjected on a daily basis on our nation's college campuses. There is a heated debate in the civil liberties community concerning the proper response to incidents of racist speech on campus.

Strong disagreements have arisen between those individuals who believe that racist speech such as that described above should be regulated by the university or some public body and those individuals who believe that racist expression should be protected from all public regulation. At the center of the controversy is a tension between the constitutional values of free speech and equality. Like the debate over affirmative action in university admissions, this issue has divided old allies and revealed unrecognized or unacknowledged differences in the experience, perceptions, and values of members of long-standing alliances. It also has caused considerable soul searching by individuals with longtime commitments to both the cause of political expression and the cause of racial equality.

I write this chapter from within the cauldron of this controversy. I make no pretense of dispassion or objectivity, but I do claim a deep commitment to the values that motivate both sides of the debate. I have spent the better part of my life as a dissenter. As a high school student I was threatened with suspension for my refusal to participate in a civil defense drill, and I have been a conspicuous consumer of my first amendment liberties ever since. I also have experienced the injury of the historical, ubiquitous, and continuous defamation of American racism. I grew up with Little Black Sambo and Amos and Andy, and I continue to receive racist tracts in the mail and shoved under my door. As I struggle with the tension between these constitutional values, I particularly appreciate the experience of both belonging and not belonging that gives to African Americans and other outsider groups a sense of duality. W.E.B. DuBois—scholar and founder of the National Association for the Advancement of Colored People (NAACP)—called the gift and burden inherent in the dual, conflicting heritage of all African Americans their "second-sight."[1]

The double consciousness of groups outside the ethnic mainstream is particularly apparent in the context of this controversy. Blacks know and value the protection the first amendment affords those of us who must rely upon our voices to petition both government and our neighbors for redress of grievances. Our political tradition has looked to "the word,"[2] to the moral power of ideas, to change the system when neither the power of the vote nor that of the gun were available. This part of us has known the experience of belonging and recognizes our common and inseparable interest in preserving the right of free speech for all. But we also know the experience of the outsider. The framers excluded us from the protection of the first amendment. The same Constitution that established rights for others endorsed a story that proclaimed our inferiority. It is a story that remains deeply ingrained in the American psyche. We see a different world than that seen by Americans who do not share this historical experience. We often hear racist speech when our white neighbors are not aware of its presence.

It is not my purpose to belittle or trivialize the importance of defending unpopular speech against the tyranny of the majority. There are very strong reasons for protecting even racist speech. Perhaps the most important reasons are that it reinforces our society's commitment to the value of tolerance, and that by shielding racist speech from government regulation, we are forced to combat it as a community. These reasons for protecting racist speech should not be set aside hastily, and I will not argue that we should be less vigilant in protecting the speech and associational rights of speakers with whom most of us would disagree.

But I am deeply concerned about the role that many civil libertarians have played, or the roles we have failed to play, in the continuing, real-life struggle through which we define the community in which we live. I fear that by framing the debate as we have—as one in which the liberty of free speech is in conflict with the elimination of racism—we have advanced the cause of racial oppression and placed the bigot on the moral high ground, fanning the rising flames of racism. Above all, I am troubled that we have not listened to the real victims, that we have shown so little empathy or understanding for their injury, and that we have abandoned those individuals whose race, gender, or sexual orientation provokes others to regard them as second-class citizens. These individuals' civil liberties are most directly at stake in the debate. In this chapter I focus on racism. Although I will not address violent pornography and homophobic hate speech directly, I will draw on the experience of women and gays as victims of hate speech where they operate as instructive analogues.

I have set two goals in constructing this chapter. The first goal is limited and perhaps overly modest, but it is nonetheless extremely important: I will demonstrate that much of the argument for protecting racist speech is based on the distinction that many civil libertarians draw between direct, face-to-face racial insults, which they think deserve first amendment protection, and all other fighting words, which they find unprotected by the first amendment. I argue that the distinction is false, that it advances none of the purposes of the first amendment, and that the time has come to put an end to the ringing rhetoric that condemns all efforts to regulate racist speech, even narrowly drafted provisions aimed at racist speech that results in direct, immediate, and substantial injury.

I also urge the regulation of racial epithets and vilification that do not involve face-to-face encounters—situations in which the victim is part of a captive audience and the injury is experienced by all members of a racial group who are forced to hear or see these words. In such cases, the insulting words are aimed at an entire group with the effect of causing significant harm to individual group members.

My second goal is more ambitious and more indeterminate. I propose several ways in which the traditional civil liberties position on free speech does not take into account important values expressed elsewhere in the Constitution. Further, I argue that even those values the first amendment itself is intended to promote are frustrated by an interpretation that is acontextual and idealized, by presupposing a world characterized by equal opportunity and the absence of societally created and culturally ingrained racism.

This chapter is divided into four parts: The first part explores whether our Constitution already commits us to some regulation of racist speech. I argue that it does; that this is the meaning of *Brown v. Board of Education*.[3] For the time being, I would ask only that the reader be open to considering this interpretation of *Brown*. This interpretation is useful even for those who believe the censorship of any expression cannot ultimately be condoned: *Brown* can help us better understand the injury of racist speech, an understanding that is vital to our discussion.

I also consider the implications of the state action doctrine in understanding *Brown* and argue that the public/private ideology promoted by that doctrine plays a critical role in advancing racism and clouding our vision of the appropriate role for the community in disestablishing systematic, societal group defamation.

The second part considers the debate over regulation of racial harassment on campus. I argue that carefully drafted regulations can and should be sustained without significant departures from existing first amendment doctrine. The regulation of racist fighting words should not be treated differently from the regulation of garden-variety fighting words, and captive audiences deserve no less protection when they are held captive by racist speakers. I also suggest that rules requiring civility and respect in academic discourse encourage rather than discourage the fullest exchange of ideas. Regulations that require minimal civility of discourse in certain designated forums are not incursions on intellectual and political debate.

The third part explores the nature of the injury inflicted by racist hate speech and examines the unstated assumptions that lie at the core of first amendment theory. In this part, I urge reconsideration of the history of racism in the United States; the ubiquity and continued vitality of culturally engendered conscious and unconscious beliefs about the inferiority of nonwhites, and the effect of inequities of power on the marketplace of ideas.

In the last part, I argue that civil libertarians must examine not just the substance of our position on racist speech but also the ways in which we enter the debate. The way the debate has been framed makes heroes out of bigots and fans the flames of racial violence. I also consider the reasons for some civil libertarians' resistance to even minimal and narrowly drafted regulations of racist harassment.

Brown v. Board of Education:
A Case About Regulating Racist Speech

The landmark case of *Brown v. Board of Education* is not one we normally think of as concerning speech. As read most narrowly, the case is about the rights of Black children to equal educational opportunity. But *Brown* can also be read more broadly to articulate a principle central to any substantive understanding of the equal protection clause, the foundation on which all anti-discrimination law rests. This is the principle of equal citizenship. Under that principle, "Every individual is presumptively entitled to be treated by the organized society as a respected, responsible, and participating member."[4] The principle further requires the affirmative disestablishment of societal practices that treat people as members of an inferior or dependent caste, as unworthy to participate in the larger community. The holding in *Brown*—that racially segregated schools violate the equal protection clause—reflects the fact that segregation amounts to a demeaning, caste-creating practice. The prevention of stigma was at the core of the Supreme Court's unanimous decision in *Brown* that segregated public schools are inherently unequal. Observing that the segregation of Black pupils "generates a feeling of inferiority as to their status in the community,"[5] Chief Justice Earl Warren recognized what a majority of the Court had ignored almost sixty years earlier in *Plessy v. Ferguson*.[6] The social meaning of racial segregation in the United States is the designation of a superior and an inferior caste, and segregation proceeds "on the ground that colored citizens are . . . inferior and degraded."[7]

The key to this understanding of *Brown* is that the practice of segregation, the practice the Court held inherently unconstitutional, was *speech. Brown* held that segregation is unconstitutional not simply because the physical separation of Black and white children is bad or because resources were distributed unequally among Black and white schools. *Brown* held that segregated schools were unconstitutional primarily because of the *message* segregation conveys—the message that Black children are an untouchable caste, unfit to be educated with white children. Segregation serves its purpose by conveying an idea. It stamps a badge of inferiority upon Blacks, and this badge communicates a message to others in the community, as well as to Blacks wearing the badge, that is injurious to Blacks. Therefore, *Brown* may be read as regulating the content of racist speech. As a regulation of racist speech, the decision is an exception to the usual rule that regulation of speech content is presumed unconstitutional.

The Conduct/Speech Distinction

Some civil libertarians argue that my analysis of *Brown* conflates speech and conduct. They maintain that the segregation outlawed in *Brown* was discriminatory conduct, not speech, and the defamatory message conveyed by segregation simply was an incidental by-product of that conduct. This position is often stated as follows: "Of course segregation conveys a message, but this could be said of almost all conduct. To take an extreme example, a murderer conveys a message of hatred for his victim. But we would not argue that we cannot punish the murder—the primary conduct—merely because of this message, which is its secondary by-product."[8] The Court has been reluctant to concede that the first amendment has any relevance whatsoever in examples like this one, because the law would not be directed at anything resembling speech or at the views expressed. In such a case the regulation of speech is truly incidental to the regulation of the conduct.

These same civil libertarians assert that I suggest that all conduct with an expressive component should be treated alike—namely, as unprotected speech. This reading of my position clearly misperceives the central point of my argument. I do not contend that *all* conduct with an expressive component should be treated as unprotected speech. To the contrary, my suggestion that *racist* conduct amounts to speech is premised upon a unique characteristic of racism—namely its reliance upon the defamatory message of white supremacy to achieve its injurious purpose. I have not ignored the distinction between the speech and conduct elements of segregation, although, as the constitutional scholar Lawrence Tribe explained, "Any particular course of conduct may be hung almost randomly on the 'speech' peg or the 'conduct' peg as one sees fit."[9] Rather, my analysis turns on that distinction; I ask the question of whether there is a purpose to outlawing segregation that is unrelated to its message and conclude that the answer is no.

If, for example, John W. Davis, counsel for the Board of Education of Topeka, Kansas, had been asked during oral argument in *Brown* to state the board's purpose in educating Black and white children in separate schools, he would have been hard pressed to answer in a way unrelated to the purpose of designating Black children as inferior. If segregation's primary goal is to convey the message of white supremacy, then *Brown's* declaration that segregation is unconstitutional amounts to a regulation of the message of white supremacy. Properly understood, *Brown* and its progeny require that the systematic group defamation of segregation be disestablished. Although the exclusion of Black children from white schools and the denial of educational resources and association that accompany exclusion can be characterized as conduct, these particular instances of conduct are concerned primarily with communicating the idea of white supremacy. The nonspeech elements are by-products of the main message rather than the message being simply a by-product of unlawful conduct.

The public accommodations provisions of the Civil Rights Act of 1964[10] illuminate why laws against discrimination also regulate racist speech. The legislative history and the Supreme Court's opinions upholding the act establish that Congress was concerned that Blacks have access to public accommodations to eliminate impediments to the free flow of interstate commerce, but this purpose could have been achieved through a regime of separate but equal accommodations. Title II of the Civil Rights Act goes farther; it incorporates the principle of the inherent inequality of segregation and prohibits restaurant owners from providing separate places at the lunch counter for "whites" and "coloreds." Even if the same food and the same service are provided, separate but equal facilities are unlawful. If the signs indicating separate facilities remain in place, then the statute is violated despite proof that restaurant patrons are free to disregard the signs. Outlawing these signs graphically illustrates my point that antidiscrimination laws are primarily regulations of the content of racist speech.

In the summer of 1966, Robert Cover and I were working as summer interns with C. B. King in Albany, Georgia. One day we stopped for lunch at a take-out chicken joint. The establishment was housed in a long diner-like structure with an awning extending from each of two doors in the side of the building. A sign was painted at the end of each awning. One said White, the other Colored. Bob and I entered the "white" side together, knowing we were not welcome to do so. When the proprietor took my order, I asked if he knew that the signs on his awnings were illegal under Title II of the Civil Rights Act of 1964. He responded, "People can come in this place through any door they want to." What this story makes apparent is that the signs themselves violate the antidiscrimination principle even when the conduct of denial of access is not present.

Another way to understand the inseparability of racist speech and discriminatory conduct is to view individual racist acts as part of a totality. When viewed in this manner, white supremacists' conduct or speech is forbidden by the equal protection clause. The goal of white supremacy is not achieved by individual acts or even by the cumulative acts of a group, but rather it is achieved by the institutionalization of the ideas of white supremacy. The institutionalization of white supremacy within our culture has created conduct on the societal level that is greater than the sum of individual racist acts. The racist acts of millions of individuals are mutually reinforcing and cumulative because the status quo of institutionalized white supremacy remains long after deliberate racist actions subside.

Professor Kendall Thomas describes the way in which racism is simultaneously speech (a socially constructed meaning or idea) and conduct by asking us to consider the concept of "race" not as a noun but as a verb. He notes that race is a social construction. The meaning of "Black" or "white" is derived through a history of acted-upon ideology. Moreover, the cultural meaning of race is promulgated through millions of ongoing contemporaneous speech/acts. Thus, he says, "We are raced." The social construction of race is an ongoing process.[11]

It is difficult to recognize the institutional significance of white supremacy or how it *acts* to harm, partially because of its ubiquity. We simply do not see most racist conduct because we experience a world in which whites are supreme as simply "the world." Much racist conduct is considered unrelated to race or regarded as neutral because racist conduct maintains the status quo, the status quo of the world as we have known it. Catharine MacKinnon has observed that "To the extent that pornography succeeds in constructing social reality, it becomes invisible as harm." Thus, pornography "is more act-like than thought-like."[12] This truth about gender discrimination is equally true of racism.

Just because one can express the idea or message embodied by a practice such as white supremacy does not necessarily equate that practice with the idea. Slavery was an idea as well as a practice, but the Supreme Court recognized the inseparability of idea and practice in the institution of slavery when it held the enabling clause of the thirteenth amendment clothed Congress with the power to pass "all laws necessary and proper for abolishing all badges and incidents of slavery in the United States."[13] This understanding also informs the regulation of speech/conduct in the public accommodations provisions of the Civil Rights Act of 1964 discussed above. When the racist restaurant or hotel owner puts a Whites Only sign in his window, his sign is more than speech. Putting up the sign is more than an act excluding Black patrons who see the sign. The sign is part of the larger practice of segregation and white supremacy that constructs and maintains a culture in which nonwhites are excluded from full citizenship. The inseparability of the idea and practice of racism is central to *Brown*'s holding that segregation is inherently unconstitutional.

Racism is both 100 percent speech and 100 percent conduct. Discriminatory conduct is not racist unless it also conveys the message of white supremacy—unless it is interpreted within the culture to advance the structure and ideology of white supremacy. Likewise, all racist speech constructs the social reality that constrains the liberty of nonwhites because of their race. By limiting the life opportunities of others, this act of constructing meaning also makes racist speech conduct.

The Public/Private Distinction

There are critics who would contend that *Brown* is inapposite because the equal protection clause only restricts government behavior, whereas the first amendment protects the speech of private persons. They say, "Of course we want to prevent the state from defaming Blacks, but we must continue to be vigilant about protecting speech rights, even of racist individuals, from the government. In both cases our concern must be protecting the individual from the unjust power of the state."

At first blush, this position seems persuasive, but its persuasiveness relies upon the mystifying properties of constitutional ideology. In particular, I refer to the state action doctrine. Roughly stated,

> The [state action] doctrine holds that although someone may have suffered harmful treatment of a kind that one might ordinarily describe as a deprivation of liberty or a denial of equal protection of the laws, that occurrence excites no constitutional concern unless the proximate active perpetrators of the harm include persons exercising the special authority or power of the government of a state.[14]

By restricting the application of the fourteenth amendment to discrimination implicating the government, the state action rule immunizes private discriminators from constitutional scrutiny. In so doing, it leaves untouched the largest part of the vast system of segregation in the United States. The *Civil Rights Cases*[15] in which this doctrine was firmly established stands as a monument preserving American racial discrimination. Although the origin of state action is textual, countervailing values of privacy, freedom of association, and free speech all have been used to justify the rule's exculpation of private racism.

For example, it is argued that a white family's decision to send its children to private school or to move to a racially exclusive suburb should be accorded respect in spite of the fourteenth amendment's requirement of nondiscrimination because these decisions are part of the right to individual familial autonomy. In this way, the state action rule's rather arbitrary limit on the scope of the antidiscrimination principle is transformed into a right of privacy—which is presented as the constitutional embodiment of an affirmative, neutral, and universally shared value. A new and positive image emerges—an image that has been abstracted from its original context.

In the abstract, the right to make decisions about how we will educate our children or with whom we will associate is an important value in American society. But when we decontextualize by viewing this privacy value in the abstract, we ignore the way it operates in the real world. We do not ask ourselves, for example, whether it is a value to which all people have equal access. And we do not inquire about who has the resources to send their children to private school or move to an exclusive suburb. The privacy value, when presented as an ideal, seems an appropriate limitation on racial justice because we naively believe that everyone has an equal stake in this value.

I do not mean to suggest that privacy or autonomy has no normative value; there is some point at which the balance ought to be struck in its favor *after full consideration of the inequities that might accompany that choice.* What is objectionable about the privacy language that I am discussing here is that it ignores inequities and assumes we all share equally in the value being promoted.

The Supreme Court's treatment of the abortion controversy provides the most striking example of the fact that the right of autonomous choice is not shared by rich and poor alike. In *Roe v. Wade*, the Court declared in no uncertain terms that the right of privacy "is broad enough to encompass a woman's decision whether or not to terminate her pregnancy."[16] Yet, in *Harris v. McRae*, the Court with equal certainty asserted, "It simply does not follow that a woman's freedom of choice carries with it a constitutional entitlement to the financial resources to avail herself of the full range of protected choices."[17]

The argument that distinguishes private racist speech from the government speech outlawed by *Brown* suffers from the same decontextualizing ideology. If the government is involved in a joint venture with private contractors to engage in the business of defaming Blacks, should it be able to escape the constitutional mandate that makes that business illegal simply by handing over the copyright and the printing presses to its partners in crime? I think not. And yet this is the essence of the position that espouses first amendment protection for those partners.

In an insightful article considering the constitutional implications of government regulation of pornography, the legal scholar Frank Michelman observed that the idea of state action plays a crucial, if unspoken, role for judges and civil libertarians who favor an absolute rule against government regulation of private pornographic publications (or racist speech), even when that expression causes "effects fairly describable . . . as deprivations of liberty and denials of equal protection of the laws."[18] He noted that judges and civil libertarians would not balance the evils of private subversions of liberty and equal protection against the evils of government censorship because "the Constitution, through the state action doctrine, in effect tells them not to." Michelman suggests that the state action doctrine, by directing us to the text of the fourteenth amendment, diverts our attention from the underlying issue—whether we should balance the evils of private deprivations of liberty against the government deprivations of liberty that may arise out of state regulations designed to avert those private deprivations.

A person who responds to the argument that *Brown* mandates the abolition of racist speech by reciting the state action doctrine fails to consider that the alternative to regulating racist speech is infringement of the claims of Blacks to liberty and equal protection. The best way to constitutionally protect these competing interests is to balance them directly. To invoke the state action doctrine is to circumvent our value judgment as to how these competing interests should be balanced.

The deference usually given to the first amendment values in this balance is justified using the argument that racist speech is unpopular speech, that like the speech of civil rights activists, pacifists, and religious and political dissenters, it is in need of special protection from majoritarian censorship. But for over three hundred years, racist speech has been the liturgy of the leading established religion of the United States, the religion of racism.

Racist speech remains a vital and regrettably popular characteristic of the U.S. vernacular. It must be noted that there has not yet been satisfactory retraction of the government-sponsored defamation in the slavery clauses,[19] the *Dred Scott* decision,[20] the Black codes, the segregation statutes, and countless other group libels. The injury to Blacks is hardly redressed by deciding the government must no longer injure our reputation if one then invokes the first amendment to ensure that racist speech continues to thrive in an unregulated private market.

Consider, for example, the case of *McLaurin v. Oklahoma State Regents*,[21] in which the University of Oklahoma graduate school, under order by a federal court to admit McLaurin, a Black student, designated a special seat, roped off from other seats, in each classroom, the library, and the cafeteria. The Supreme Court held that this arrangement was unconstitutional because McLaurin could not have had an equal opportunity to learn and participate if he was humiliated and symbolically stigmatized as an untouchable. Would it be any less injurious if all McLaurin's classmates had shown up at class wearing blackface? Should this symbolic speech be protected by the Constitution? Yet, according to a *Time* magazine report, in the fall of 1988 at the University of Wisconsin, "Members of the Zeta Beta Tau fraternity staged a mock slave auction, complete with some pledges in blackface."[22] More recently, at the same university, white male students trailed Black female students shouting, "I've never tried a nigger before."[23] These young women were no less severely injured than was McLaurin simply because the university did not directly sponsor their assault. If the university fails to protect them in their right to pursue their education free from this kind of degradation and humiliation, then surely there are constitutional values at stake.

It is a very sad irony that the first instinct of many civil libertarians is to express concern for possible infringement of the assailants' liberties while barely noticing the constitutional rights of the assailed. Shortly after *Brown*, many Southern communities tried to escape the mandate of desegregation by closing public schools and opening private (white) academies. These attempts to avoid the fourteenth amendment through the privatization of discrimination consistently were invalidated by the courts. In essence, the Supreme Court held that the defamatory message of segregation would not be insulated from constitutional proscription simply because the speaker was a nongovernment entity.

The Supreme Court also has indicated that Congress may enact legislation regulating private racist speech. In upholding the public accommodations provisions of Title II of the Civil Rights Act of 1964 in *Heart of Atlanta Motel v. United States*,[24] the Court implicitly rejected the argument that the absence of state action meant that private discriminators were protected by first amendment free speech and associational rights. Likewise in *Bob Jones University v. United States,*[25] the Court sustained the Internal Revenue Service decision to discontinue tax-exempt status for a college with a policy against interracial dating and marriage. The college framed its objection in terms of the free exercise of religion, arguing its policy was religiously motivated, but the Court found that the government had "a fundamental, overriding interest in eradicating racial discrimination in education" that "substantially outweighs whatever burden denial of tax benefits" placed on the college's exercise of its religious beliefs.[26] It is difficult to believe that the university would have fared any better under free speech analysis or if the policy had been merely a statement of principle rather than an enforceable disciplinary regulation. Regulation of private racist speech also has been held constitutional in the context of prohibition of race-designated advertisements for employees, home sales, and rentals.

Thus *Brown* and the antidiscrimination law it spawned provide precedent for my position that the content regulation of racist speech is not only permissible but may be required by the Constitution in certain circumstances. This precedent may not mean that we should advocate the government regulation of all racist speech, but it should give us pause in assuming absolutist positions about regulations aimed at the message or idea such speech conveys. If we understand *Brown*—the cornerstone of the civil rights movement and equal protection doctrine—correctly, and if we understand the necessity of disestablishing the system of signs and symbols that signal Blacks' inferiority, then we should not proclaim that all racist speech that stops short of physical violence must be defended.

Racist Speech as the Functional Equivalent of Fighting Words

Much recent debate over the efficacy of regulating racist speech has focused on the efforts by colleges and universities to respond to the burgeoning incidents of racial harassment on their campuses. At Stanford, where I teach, there has been considerable controversy over whether racist and other discriminatory verbal harassment should be regulated and what form any regulation should take. Proponents of regulation have been sensitive to the danger of inhibiting expression, and the current regulation (which was drafted by my colleague Tom Grey) manifests that sensitivity. It is drafted somewhat more narrowly than I would have preferred, leaving unregulated hate speech that occurs in settings where there is a captive audience, but I largely agree with this regulation's substance and approach. I include it here as one example of a regulation of racist speech that I would argue violates neither first amendment precedent nor principle. The regulation reads as follows:

Fundamental Standard Interpretation: Free Expression and Discriminatory Harassment

1. Stanford is committed to the principles of free inquiry and free expression. Students have the right to hold and vigorously defend and promote their opinions, thus entering them into the life of the University, there to flourish or wither according to their merits. Respect for this right requires that students tolerate even expression of opinions which they find abhorrent. Intimidation of students by other students in their exercise of this right, by violence or threat of violence, is therefore considered to be a violation of the Fundamental Standard.

2. Stanford is also committed to principles of equal opportunity and non-discrimination. Each student has the right to equal access to a Stanford education, without discrimination on the basis of sex, race, color, handicap, religion, sexual orientation, or national and ethnic origin. Harassment of students on the basis of any of these characteristics tends to create a hostile environment that makes access to education for those subjected to it less than equal. Such discriminatory harassment is therefore considered to be a violation of the Fundamental Standard.

3. This interpretation of the Fundamental Standard is intended to clarify the point at which protected free expression ends and prohibited discriminatory harassment begins. Prohibited harassment includes discriminatory intimidation by threats of violence, and also includes personal vilification of students on the basis of their sex, race, color, handicap, religion, sexual orientation, or national and ethnic origin.

4. Speech or other expression constitutes harassment by vilification if it:

   a) is intended to insult or stigmatize an individual or a small number of individuals on the basis of their sex, race, color, handicap, religion, sexual orientation, or national and ethnic origin; and

   b) is addressed directly to the individual or individuals whom it insults or stigmatizes; and

   c) makes use of "fighting" words or non-verbal symbols.

   In the context of discriminatory harassment, "fighting" words or non-verbal symbols are words, pictures or symbols that, by virtue of their form, are commonly understood to convey direct and visceral hatred or contempt for human beings on the basis of their sex, race, color, handicap, religion, sexual orientation, and national and ethnic origin.[27]

This regulation and others like it have been characterized in the press as the work of "thought police," but the rule does nothing more than prohibit intentional face-to-face insults, a form of speech that is unprotected by the first amendment. When racist speech takes the form of face-to-face insults, catcalls, or other assaultive speech aimed at an individual or a small group of persons, then it falls within the "fighting words" exception to first amendment protection. The Supreme Court has held that words that "by their very utterance inflict injury or tend to incite an immediate breach of the peace"[28] are not constitutionally protected.

Face-to-face racial insults, like fighting words, are undeserving of first amendment protection for two reasons. The first reason is the immediacy of the injurious impact of racial insults. The experience of being called "nigger," "spic," "Jap," or "kike" is like receiving a slap in the face. The injury is instantaneous. There is neither an opportunity for intermediary reflection on the idea conveyed nor an opportunity for responsive speech. The harm to be avoided is both clear and present. The second reason that racial insults should not fall under protected speech relates to the purpose underlying the first amendment. The purpose of the first amendment is to foster the greatest amount of speech. Racial insults disserve that purpose. Assaultive racist speech functions as a preemptive strike. The racial invective is experienced as a blow, not a proffered idea, and once the blow is struck, it is unlikely that dialogue will follow. Racial insults are undeserving of first amendment protection because the perpetrator's intention is not to discover truth or initiate dialogue, but to injure the victim.

The fighting words doctrine anticipates that the verbal slap in the face of insulting words will provoke a violent response, resulting in a breach of the peace. When racial insults are hurled at minorities, the response may be silence or flight rather than a fight, but the preemptive effect on further speech is the same. Women and minorities often report that they find themselves speechless in the face of discriminatory verbal attacks. This inability to respond is not the result of oversensitivity among these groups, as some individuals who oppose protective regulation have argued. Rather it is the product of several factors, all of which evidence the nonspeech character of the initial preemptive verbal assault. The first factor is that the visceral emotional response to personal attack precludes speech. Attack produces an instinctive, defensive psychological reaction. Fear, rage, shock, and flight all interfere with any reasoned response. Words like "nigger," "kike," and "faggot" produce physical symptoms that temporarily disable the victim, and the perpetrators often use these words with the intention of producing this effect. Many victims do not find words of response until well after the assault, when the cowardly assaulter has departed.

A second factor that distinguishes racial insults from protected speech is the preemptive nature of such insults—words of response to such verbal attacks may never be forthcoming because speech is usually an inadequate response. When one is personally attacked with words that denote one's sub-human status and untouchability, there is little, if anything, that can be said to redress either the emotional or reputational injury. This is particularly true when the message and meaning of the epithet resonates with beliefs widely held in society. This preservation of widespread beliefs is what makes the face-to-face racial attack more likely to preempt speech than other fighting words do. The racist name caller is accompanied by a cultural chorus of equally demeaning speech and symbols. Segregation and other forms of racist speech injure victims because of their dehumanizing and excluding message. Each individual message gains its power because of the cumulative and reinforcing effect of countless similar messages that are conveyed in a society where racism is ubiquitous.

The subordinated victims of fighting words also are silenced by their relatively powerless position in society. Because of the significance of power and position, the categorization of racial epithets as fighting words provides an inadequate paradigm; instead one must speak of their functional equivalent. The fighting words doctrine presupposes an encounter between two persons of relatively equal power who have been acculturated to respond to face-to-face insults with violence: The fighting words doctrine is a paradigm based on a white male point of view. It captures the "macho" quality of male discourse. It is accepted, justifiable, and even praiseworthy when "real men" respond to personal insult with violence. (Presidential candidate George Bush effectively emulated the most macho—and not coincidentally most violent—of movie stars, Clint Eastwood, when he repeatedly used the phrase, "Read my lips!" Any teenage boy will tell you the subtext of this message: "I've got nothing else to say about this and if you don't like what I'm saying we can step outside.") The fighting words doctrine's responsiveness to this male stance in the world and its blindness to the cultural experience of women is another example of how neutral principles of law reflect the values of those who are dominant.

Black men also are well aware of the double standard that our culture applies in responding to insult. Part of the culture of racial domination through violence—a culture of dominance manifested historically in thousands of lynchings in the South and more recently in the racial violence at Howard Beach and Bensonhurst—is the paradoxical expectation on the part of whites that Black males will accept insult from whites without protest, yet will become violent without provocation. These expectations combine two assumptions: First, that Blacks as a group—and especially Black men—are more violent; and second, that as inferior persons, Blacks have no right to feel insulted. One can imagine the response of universities if Black men started to respond to racist fighting words by beating up white students.

In most situations, minorities correctly perceive that a violent response to fighting words will result in a risk to their own life and limb. This risk forces targets to remain silent and submissive. This response is most obvious when women submit to sexually assaultive speech or when the racist name caller is in a more powerful position—the boss on the job or a member of a violent racist group. Certainly, we do not expect the Black woman crossing the Wisconsin campus to turn on her tormentors and pummel them. Less obvious, but just as significant, is the effect of pervasive racial and sexual violence and coercion on individual members of subordinated groups, who must learn the survival techniques of suppressing and disguising rage and anger at an early age.

One of my students, a white, gay male, related an experience that is quite instructive in understanding the fighting words doctrine. In response to my request that students describe how they experienced the injury of racist speech, Michael told a story of being called "faggot" by a man on a subway. His description included all of the speech-inhibiting elements I have noted previously. He found himself in a state of semishock, nauseous, dizzy, unable to muster the witty, sarcastic, articulate rejoinder he was accustomed to making. He was instantly aware of the recent spate of gay bashing in San Francisco and that many of these incidents had escalated from verbal encounters. Even hours later when the shock subsided and his facility with words returned, he realized that any response was inadequate to counter the hundreds of years of societal defamation that one word—"faggot"—carried with it. Like the word "nigger" and unlike the word "liar," it is not sufficient to deny the truth of the word's application, to say, "I am not a faggot." One must deny the truth of the word's meaning, a meaning shouted from the rooftops by the rest of the world a million times a day. The complex response "Yes, I am a member of the group you despise and the degraded meaning of the word you use is one that I reject" is not effective in a subway encounter. Although there are many of us who constantly and in myriad ways seek to counter the lie spoken in the meaning of hateful words like "nigger" and "faggot," it is a nearly impossible burden to bear when one is ambushed by a sudden, face-to-face hate speech assault.

But there was another part of my discussion with Michael that is equally instructive. I asked if he could remember a situation when he had been verbally attacked with reference to his being a white male. Had he ever been called a "honkey," a "chauvinist pig," or "mick"? (Michael is from a working-class Irish family in Boston.) He said that he had been called some version of all three and that although he found the last one more offensive than the first two, he had not experienced—even in that subordinated role—the same disorienting powerlessness he had experienced when attacked for his membership in the gay community. The question of power, of the context of the power relationships within which speech takes place, and the connection to violence must be considered as we decide how best to foster the freest and fullest dialogue within our communities. Regulation of face-to-face verbal assault in the manner contemplated by the proposed Stanford provision will make room for more speech than it chills. The provision is clearly within the spirit, if not the letter, of existing first amendment doctrine.

The proposed Stanford regulation, and indeed regulations with considerably broader reach, can be justified as necessary to protect a captive audience from offensive or injurious speech. Courts have held that offensive speech may not be regulated in public forums such as streets and parks where listeners may avoid the speech by moving on or averting their eyes,[29] but the regulation of otherwise protected speech has been permitted when the speech invades the privacy of unwilling listeners' homes or when unwilling listeners cannot avoid the speech.[30] Racists posters, flyers, and graffiti in dorms, classrooms, bathrooms, and other common living spaces would fall within the reasoning of these cases. Minority students should not be required to remain in their rooms to avoid racial assault. Minimally, they should find a safe haven in their dorms and other common rooms that are a part of their daily routine. I would argue that the university's responsibility for ensuring these students receive an equal educational opportunity provides a compelling justification for regulations that ensure them safe passage in all common areas. Black, Latino, Asian, or Native American students should not have to risk being the target of racially assaulting speech every time they choose to walk across campus. The regulation of vilifying speech that cannot be anticipated or avoided would not preclude announced speeches and rallies where minorities and their allies would have an opportunity to organize counterdemonstrations or avoid the speech altogether.

Knowing the Injury and Striking the Balance: Understanding What Is at Stake in Racist Speech Cases

I argued in the last section that narrowly drafted regulations of racist speech that prohibit face-to-face vilification and protect captive audiences from verbal and written harassment can be defended within the confines of existing first amendment doctrine. Here I argue that many civil libertarians who urge that the first amendment prohibits any regulation of racist speech have given inadequate attention to the testimony of individuals who have experienced injury from such speech. These civil libertarians fail to comprehend both the nature and extent of the injury inflicted by racist speech. I further urge that understanding the injury requires reconsideration of the balance that must be struck between our concerns for racial equality and freedom of expression.

The arguments most commonly advanced against the regulation of racist speech go something like this: We recognize that minority groups suffer pain and injury as the result of racist speech, but we must allow this hate mongering for the benefit of society as a whole. Freedom of speech is the lifeblood of our democratic system. It is a freedom that enables us to persuade others to our point of view. Free speech is especially important for minorities because often it is their only vehicle for rallying support for redress of their grievances. Even though we do not wish anyone to be persuaded that racist lies are true, we cannot allow the public regulation of racist invective and vilification because any prohibition broad enough to prevent racist speech would catch in the same net forms of speech that are central to a democratic society.

Whenever we argue that racist epithets and vilification must be allowed, not because we would condone them ourselves but because of the potential danger the precedent of regulation would pose for the speech of all dissenters, we are balancing our concern for the free flow of ideas and the democratic process with our desire for equality. This kind of categorical balance is struck whenever we frame any rule—even an absolute rule. It is important to be conscious of the nature and extent of injury to both concerns when we engage in this kind of balancing. In this case, we must place on one side of the balance the nature and extent of the injury caused by racism. We must also consider whether the racist speech we propose to regulate is advancing or retarding the values of the first amendment.

Understanding the Injury Inflicted by Racist Speech

There can be no meaningful discussion about how to reconcile our commitment to equality and our commitment to free speech until we acknowledge that racist speech inflicts real harm and that this harm is far from trivial. I should state that more strongly: To engage in a debate about the first amendment and racist speech without a full understanding of the nature and extent of the harm of racist speech risks making the first amendment an instrument of domination rather than a vehicle of liberation. Not everyone has known the experience of being victimized by racist, misogynist, or homophobic speech, and we do not share equally the burden of the societal harm it inflicts. Often we are too quick to say we have heard the victims' cries when we have not; we are too eager to assure ourselves we have experienced the same injury and therefore can make the constitutional balance without danger of mismeasurement. For many of us who have fought for the rights of oppressed minorities, it is difficult to accept that by underestimating the injury from racist speech we too might be implicated in the vicious words we would never utter. Until we have eradicated racism and sexism and no longer share in the fruits of those forms of domination, we cannot legitimately strike the balance without hearing the protest of those who are dominated. My plea is simply that we listen to the victims.

Members of my own family were involved in a recent incident at a private school in Wilmington, Delaware, that taught me much about both the nature of the injury racist speech inflicts and the lack of understanding many whites have of that injury.

A good Quaker school dedicated to a deep commitment to and loving concern for all the members of its community, Wilmington Friends School also became a haven for white families fleeing the court-ordered desegregation of the Wilmington public schools. In recent years, the school strove to meet its commitment to human equality by enrolling a small (but significant) group of minority students and hiring an even smaller number of Black faculty and staff. My sister Paula, a gifted, passionate, and dedicated teacher, was the principal of the lower school. Her sons attended the high school. My brother-in-law, John, teaches geology at the University of Delaware. He is a strong, quiet, loving man, and he is white. My sister's family had moved to

Wilmington, shouldering the extra burdens and anxieties borne by an inter-racial family moving to a town where, not long ago, the defamatory message of segregation graced the doors of bathrooms and restaurants. Within a year they had made a place as well-loved and respected members of the com-munity, particularly the school community, where Paula was viewed as a godsend and my nephews made many good friends.

In May of their second year in Wilmington, an incident occurred that shook the entire school community, but was particularly painful to my sister's family and others who found themselves the objects of hateful speech. In a letter to the school community explaining a decision to expel four students, the school's headmistress described the incident as follows:

> On Sunday evening, May 1, four students in the senior class met by pre-arrangement to paint the soccer kickboard, a flat rectangular structure, approximately 8 ft. by 25 ft., standing in the midst of the Wilmington Friends School playing fields. They worked for approximately one hour under bright moonlight and then went home.
>
> What confronted students and staff the following morning, depicted on the kickboard, were racist and anti-Semitic slogans and, most disturbing of all, threats of violent assault against one clearly identified member of the senior class. The slogans written on the kickboard included "Save the land, join the Klan," and "Down with Jews"; among the drawings were at least twelve hooded Ku Klux Klansmen, Nazi swastikas, and a burning cross. The most frightening and disturbing depictions, however, were those that threatened violence against one of our senior Black students. He was drawn, in a cartoon figure, identified by his name, and his initials, and by the name of his mother. Directly to the right of his head was a bullet, and farther to the right was a gun with its barrel directed toward the head. Under the drawing of the student, three Ku Klux Klansmen were depicted, one of whom was saying that the student "dies." Next to the gun was a drawing of a burning cross under which was written "Kill the Tarbaby."[31]

When I visited my sister's family a few days after this incident, the injury they had suffered was evident. The wounds were fresh. My sister, a care giver by nature and vocation, was clearly in need of care. My nephews were quiet. Their faces betrayed the aftershock of a recently inflicted blow and a newly discovered vulnerability. I knew the pain and scars were no less enduring because the injury had not been physical. And when I talked to my sister, I realized the greatest part of her pain came not from the incident itself, but rather from the reaction of white parents who had come to the school in unprecedented numbers to protest the offending students' expulsion. "It was only a prank." "No one was physically attacked." "How can you punish these kids for mere words, mere drawings." Paula's pain was compounded by the failure of these people with whom she lived and worked to recognize that she had been hurt, to understand in even the most limited way the reality of her pain and that of her family.

Many people called the incident "isolated." But Black folks know that no racial incident is "isolated" in the United States. That is what makes the incidents so horrible, so scary. It is the knowledge that they are *not* the isolated unpopular speech of a dissident few that makes them so frightening. These incidents are manifestations of an ubiquitous and deeply ingrained cultural belief system, an American way of life. Too often in recent months, as I have debated this issue with friends and colleagues, I have heard people speak of the need to protect "offensive" speech. The word offensive is used as if we were speaking of a difference in taste, as if I should learn to be less sensitive to words that "offend" me. I cannot help but believe that those people who speak of offense—those who argue that this speech must go unchecked—do not understand the great difference between offense and injury. They have not known the injury my sister experienced, have not known the fear, vulnerability, and shame experienced by the Wisconsin students described at the beginning of this chapter. There is a great difference between the offensiveness of words that you would rather not hear because they are labeled dirty, impolite, or personally demeaning and the *injury* inflicted by words that remind the world that you are fair game for physical attack, that evoke in you all of the millions of cultural lessons regarding your inferiority that you have so painstakingly repressed, and that imprint upon you a badge of servitude and subservience for all the world to see. It is instructive that the chief proponents of restricting people who inflict these injuries are women and people of color, and there are few among these groups who take the absolutist position that any regulation of this speech is too much.

Again, *Brown v. Board of Education* is a useful case for our analysis. *Brown* is helpful because it articulates the nature of the injury inflicted by the racist message of segregation. When one considers the injuries identified in the *Brown* decision, it is clear that racist speech causes tangible injury, and it is the kind of injury for which the law commonly provides, and even requires, redress.

Psychic injury is no less an injury than being struck in the face, and it often is far more severe. *Brown* speaks directly to the psychic injury inflicted by racist speech in noting that the symbolic message of segregation affected "the hearts and minds" of Negro children "in a way unlikely ever to be undone."[32] Racial epithets and harassment often cause deep emotional scarring and feelings of anxiety and fear that pervade every aspect of a victim's life. Many victims of hate propaganda have experienced physiological and emotional symptoms, such as rapid pulse rate and difficulty in breathing.

A second injury identified in *Brown,* and present in my example, is reputational injury. As Professor Tribe has noted, "Libelous speech was long regarded as a form of personal assault . . . that government could vindicate

. . . without running afoul of the constitution."[33] Although *New York Times v. Sullivan* and its progeny have subjected much defamatory speech to constitutional scrutiny—on the reasoning that "debate on public issues should be uninhibited, robust and wide-open"[34] and should not be "chilled" by the possibility of libel suits—these cases also demonstrate a concern for balancing the public's interest in being fully informed with the competing interest of defamed persons in vindicating their reputation.

The interest of defamed persons is even stronger in racial defamation cases than in the *Sullivan* line of cases. The *Sullivan* rule protects statements of fact that are later proven erroneous. But persons who defame a racial group with racial epithets and stereotyped caricatures are not concerned that they may have "guessed wrong" in attempting to ascertain the truth. The racial epithet is the expression of a widely held belief. It is invoked as an assault, not as a statement of fact that may be proven true or false. Moreover, if the *Sullivan* rule protects erroneous speech because of an ultimate concern for the discovery of truth, then the rule's application to racial epithets must be based on an acceptance of the possible "truth" of racism, a position that, happily, most first amendment absolutists are reluctant to embrace. Furthermore, the rationale of *Sullivan* and its progeny is that public issues should be vigorously debated and that, as the Supreme Court held in *Gertz v. Robert Welch, Inc.,* there is "no such thing as a false idea."[35] But are racial insults ideas? Do they encourage wide-open debate?

Brown is a case about group defamation. The message of segregation was stigmatizing to Black children. To be labeled unfit to attend school with white children injured the reputation of Black children, thereby foreclosing employment opportunities and the right to be regarded as respected members of the body politic. An extensive discussion on the constitutionality or efficacy of group libel laws is beyond the scope of this chapter, and it must suffice for me to note that although *Beauharnais v. Illinois*,[36] which upheld an Illinois group libel statute, has fallen into disfavor with some commentators, *Brown* remains an instructive case. By identifying the inseparability of discriminatory speech and action in the case of segregation, where the injury is inflicted by the meaning of the segregation, *Brown* limits the scope of *Sullivan*. *Brown* reflects the understanding that racism is a form of subordination that achieves its purposes through group defamation.

The third injury identified in *Brown* is the denial of equal educational opportunity. *Brown* recognized that even where segregated facilities are materially equal, Black children did not have an equal opportunity to learn and participate in the school community if they bore the additional burden of being subjected to the humiliation and psychic assault that accompanies the message of segregation. University students bear an analogous burden when they are forced to live and work in an environment where at any moment they may be subjected to denigrating verbal harassment and assault.

The testimony of nonwhite students about the detrimental effect of racial harassment on their academic performance and social integration in the college community is overwhelming. A similar injury is recognized and addressed in the requirement of Title VII of the Civil Rights Act that employers maintain a nondiscriminatory, nonhostile work environment and in federal and state regulations prohibiting sexual harassment on campuses as well as in the workplace.

All three of these very tangible, continuing, and often irreparable forms of injury—psychic, reputational, and the denial of equal educational opportunity—must be recognized, accounted for, and balanced against the claim that a regulation aimed at the prevention of these injuries may lead to restrictions on important first amendment liberties.

The Other Side of the Balance: Does the Suppression of Racial Epithets Weigh for or Against Speech?

In striking a balance, we also must think about what we are weighing on the side of speech. Most Blacks—unlike many white civil libertarians—do not have faith in free speech as the most important vehicle for liberation. The first amendment coexisted with slavery, and we still are not sure it will protect us to the same extent that it protects whites. It often is argued that minorities have benefited greatly from first amendment protection and therefore should guard it jealously. We are aware that the struggle for racial equality has relied heavily on the persuasion of peaceful protest protected by the first amendment, but experience also teaches us that our petitions often go unanswered until protests disrupt business as usual and require the self-interested attention of those persons in power.

Paradoxically, the disruption that renders protest speech effective usually causes it to be considered undeserving of first amendment protection. Note the cruel irony in the news story cited at the beginning of this chapter that describes the Stanford president's justification for prosecuting students engaged in a peaceful sit-in for violation of the university's Fundamental Standard: The protesting students were punished, but the racist behavior the students were protesting went unpunished. This lack of symmetry was justified on the grounds that punishment might violate the bigots' first amendment rights—a particularly ironic result given Professor Derrick Bell's observation that it was Black students' civil rights protests that underlay the precedents upon which white students relied to establish their first amendment rights in school and university settings. As in so many other areas, a policy that Blacks paid the price for is used against them and on behalf of whites. Once one begins to doubt the existence of a symmetry between official reactions to racism and official reactions to protests against racism, the absolutist position loses credence: It becomes difficult for us to believe that fighting to protect speech rights for racists will ensure our own speech rights. Our experience is that the American system of justice has never been symmetrical where race is concerned. No wonder we see equality as a pre-condition of free speech and place more weight on that side of the balance aimed at the removal of the badges and incidents of slavery that continue to flourish in our culture.

Blacks and other people of color are equally skeptical about the absolutist argument that even the most injurious speech must remain unregulated because in an unregulated marketplace of ideas the best ideas will rise to the top and gain acceptance. Our experience tells us the opposite. We have seen too many demagogues elected by appealing to U.S. racism. We have seen too many good, liberal politicians shy away from the issues that might brand them as too closely allied with us. The American marketplace of ideas was founded with the idea of the racial inferiority of nonwhites as one of its chief commodities, and ever since the market opened, racism has remained its most active item in trade.

But it is not just the prevalence and strength of the idea of racism that make the unregulated marketplace of ideas an untenable paradigm for those individuals who seek full and equal personhood for all. The real problem is that the idea of the racial inferiority of nonwhites infects, skews, and disables the operation of a market (like a computer virus, sick cattle, or diseased wheat). It trumps good ideas that contend with it in the market. It is an epidemic that distorts the marketplace of ideas and renders it dysfunctional.

Racism is irrational. Individuals do not embrace or reject racist beliefs as the result of reasoned deliberation. For the most part, we do not even recognize the myriad ways in which the racism that pervades our history and culture influences our beliefs. But racism is ubiquitous. We are all racists. Often we fail to see it because racism is so woven into our culture that it seems normal. In other words, most of our racism is unconscious. So it must have been with the middle-aged, white, male lawyer who thought he was complimenting a Mexican-American law student of mine who had applied for a job with his firm. "You speak very good English," he said. But she was a fourth-generation Californian, not the stereotypical poor immigrant he unconsciously imagined she must be.

The disruptive and disabling effect on the market of an idea that is ubiq-uitous and irrational, but seldom seen or acknowledged, should be apparent. If the community is considering competing ideas about providing food for children, shelter for the homeless, or abortions for pregnant women, and the choices made among the proposed solutions are influenced by the idea that some children, families, or women are less deserving of our sympathy because they are racially inferior, then the market is not functioning as either John Stuart Mill or Oliver Wendell Holmes envisioned it. In the term used by constitutional theorist John Ely, there is a "process defect."[37]

Professor Ely coined the term *process defect* in the context of developing a theory to identify instances in which legislative action should be subjected to heightened judicial scrutiny under the equal protection clause. Ely argued that the courts should interfere with the normal majoritarian political process when the defect of prejudice bars groups subject to widespread vilification from participation in the political process and causes governmental decisionmakers to misapprehend the costs and benefits of their actions. This same process defect that excludes vilified groups and misdirects the government operates in the marketplace of ideas. Mill's vision of truth emerging through competition in the marketplace of ideas relies on the ability of members of the body politic to recognize "truth" as serving their interest and to act on that recognition.[38] As such, this vision depends upon the same process that James Madison referred to when he described his vision of a democracy in which the numerous minorities within our society would form coalitions to create majorities with overlapping interests through pluralist wheeling and dealing.[39] Just as the defect of prejudice blinds white voters to interests that overlap with those of vilified minorities, it also blinds them to the "truth" of an idea or the efficacy of solutions associated with that vilified group. And just as prejudice causes the governmental decisionmakers to misapprehend the costs and benefits of their actions, it also causes all of us to misapprehend the value of ideas in the market.

Prejudice that is unconscious or unacknowledged causes the most significant distortions in the market. When racism operates at a conscious level, opposing ideas may prevail in open competition for the rational or moral sensibilities of the market participant. But when individuals are unaware of their prejudice, neither reason nor moral persuasion will likely succeed.

Racist speech also distorts the marketplace of ideas by muting or devaluing the speech of Blacks and other despised minorities. Regardless of intrinsic value, their words and ideas become less salable in the marketplace of ideas. An idea that would be embraced by large numbers of individuals if it were offered by a white individual will be rejected or given less credence if its author belongs to a group demeaned and stigmatized by racist beliefs.

An obvious example of this type of devaluation is the Black political candidate whose ideas go unheard or are rejected by white voters, although voters would embrace the same ideas if they were championed by a white candidate. Once again, the experience of one of my gay students provides a paradigmatic example of how ideas are less acceptable when their authors are members of a group that has been victimized by hatred and vilification. Bob had not "come out" when he first came to law school. During his first year, when issues relating to heterosexism came up in class or in discussions with other students, he spoke to these issues as a sympathetic "straight" white male student. His arguments were listened to and taken seriously. In his second year, when he had come out and his classmates knew that he was gay, he found that he was not nearly as persuasive an advocate for his position as when he was identified as straight. He was the same person saying the same things, but his identity gave him less authority. Similarly, Catharine MacKinnon argues that pornography causes women to be taken less seriously as they enter the public arena.[40] Racial minorities have the same experiences on a daily basis as they endure the microaggression of having their words doubted, or misinterpreted, or assumed to be without evidentiary support, or when their insights are ignored and then appropriated by whites who are assumed to have been the original authority.

Finally, racist speech decreases the total amount of speech that reaches the market by coercively silencing members of those groups who are its targets. I noted earlier in this chapter the ways in which racist speech is inextricably linked with racist conduct. The primary purpose and effect of the speech/conduct that constitutes white supremacy is the exclusion of nonwhites from full participation in the body politic. Sometimes the speech/conduct of racism is direct and obvious. When the Klan burns a cross on the lawn of a Black person who joined the NAACP or exercised the right to move to a formerly all-white neighborhood, the effect of this speech does not result from the persuasive power of an idea operating freely in the market. It is a threat; a threat made in the context of a history of lynchings, beatings, and economic reprisals that made good on earlier threats; a threat that silences a potential speaker. Such a threat may be difficult to recognize because the tie between the speech and the threatened act is unstated. The tie does not need to be explicit because the promised violence is systemic. The threat is effective because racially motivated violence is a well-known historical and contemporary reality. The threat may be even more effective than a phone call that takes responsibility for a terrorist bomb attack and promises another, a situation in which we easily recognize the inextricable link between the speech and the threatened act. The Black student who is subjected to racial epithets, like the Black person on whose lawn the Klan has burned a cross, is threatened and silenced by a credible connection between racist hate speech and racist violence. Certainly the recipients of hate speech may be uncommonly brave or foolhardy and ignore the system of violence in which this abusive speech is only a bit player. But it is more likely that we, as a community, will be denied the benefit of many of their thoughts and ideas.

Again MacKinnon's analysis of how first amendment law misconstrues pornography is instructive. She notes that in concerning themselves only with government censorship, first amendment absolutists fail to recognize that whole segments of the population are systematically silenced by powerful private actors. "As a result, [they] cannot grasp that the speech of some silences the speech of others in a way that is not simply a matter of competition for airtime."[41]

Asking Victim Groups to Pay the Price

Whenever we decide that racist hate speech must be tolerated because of the importance of tolerating unpopular speech, we ask Blacks and other subordinated groups to bear a burden for the good of society—to pay the price for the societal benefit of creating more room for speech. And we assign this burden to them without seeking their advice or consent. This amounts to white domination, pure and simple. It is taxation without representation. We must be careful that the ease with which we strike the balance against the regulation of racist speech is in no way influenced by the fact the cost will be borne by others. We must be certain that the individuals who pay the price are fairly represented in our deliberation and that they are heard.

Even as our discussions concerning the efficacy of regulating racist speech on campuses continue, they evidence our lack of attention to the costs of constitutional injury borne by the victims. I have had scores of conversations about this topic over the past several months with students, colleagues, university administrators, ACLU board members, reporters, friends, relatives, and strangers. By now there is an experience of déjà vu each time I am asked to explain how a good civil libertarian like myself—a veteran of 1960s sit-ins and demonstrations, a progressive constitutional law professor, and a person who has made antiestablishment speech his vocation—could advocate censorship. I try to be patient, articulate, and good natured as I set forth the concerns and arguments explored in this chapter. I try to listen carefully, to remain open to others' experiences and to my own strong instincts against governmental incursion on individual liberty.

Often when I am at my best, even the most steadfast defenders of the first amendment faith will concede that these are persuasive arguments. They say they agree with much of what I have said, they recognize I am proposing narrowly framed restrictions on only the most abusive, least substantive forms of racist speech, and they understand the importance of hearing the victims' stories. Then they say, "But I'm afraid I still come out differently from you in the end. I still don't see how we can allow even this limited regulation of racist speech without running some risk of endangering our first amendment liberties."

One of these encounters occurred at a recent dinner with colleagues in New York. My good friend and former colleague john powell—john is national legal director of the ACLU and he is Black—was in attendance. He told the following story:

> My family was having Thanksgiving dinner at the home of friends. We are vegetarians and my two kids were trying to figure out which of the two dressings on the table was the vegetarian dressing and which was the meat dressing. One of our hosts pointed to one of the dressings and said, "This is the regular dressing and the other is the vegetarian dressing." I corrected him

saying, "There is no such thing as 'regular' dressing. There is meat dressing and there is vegetarian dressing, but neither one of them is regular dressing."

This incident reminded powell of the discussions he has had with his colleagues on the subject of regulating racist speech. "Somehow," he said,

> I always come away from these discussions feeling that my white colleagues think about the first amendment the way my friend thought about "regular" [meat] dressing, as an amendment for regular people or all people, and that they think of the equal protection clause of the fourteenth amendment the way my friend thought about vegetarian dressing, as a special amendment for a minority of different people.

Inevitably, in these conversations, those of us who are nonwhite bear the burden of justification, of justifying our concern for protection under our "special" amendment. It is not enough that we have demonstrated tangible and continuing injury committed against the victims of racist speech. There can be no public remedy for our special fourteenth amendment injury until we have satisfied our interlocutors that there is no possible risk of encroachment on their first amendment—the "regular" amendment.

If one asks why we always begin by asking whether we can afford to fight racism rather than asking whether we can afford not to, or if one asks why my colleagues who oppose all regulation of racist speech do not feel that the burden is theirs to justify a reading of the first amendment that requires sacrificing rights guaranteed under the equal protection clause, then one sees an example of how unconscious racism operates in the marketplace of ideas.

Well-meaning individuals who are committed to equality without regard to race and who have demonstrated that commitment in many arenas do not recognize where the burden of persuasion has been placed in this discussion. When they do, they do not understand why. Even as I experienced the frustration of always bearing the burden of persuasion, I did not see the source of my frustration or understand its significance until powell told his story about the Thanksgiving dressing. Unfortunately, our unconscious racism causes even those of us who are the direct victims of racism to view the first amendment as the "regular" amendment—an amendment that works for all people—and the equal protection clause and racial equality as a special-interest amendment important to groups that are less valued.

Derrick Bell has noted that often in our constitutional history the rights of Blacks have been sacrificed because sacrifice was believed necessary to preserve the greater interests of the whole.[42] It is not just the actual sacrifice that is racist but also the way the "whole with the greater interests" gets defined. Today in a world committed to the idea of equality, we rarely notice the sacrifice or how we have avoided noticing the sacrifice by defining the interests of whites as the whole, "the regular." When we think this way, when we see the potential danger of incursions on the first amendment but do not see existing incursions on the fourteenth amendment, our perceptions have been influenced by an entire belief system that makes us less sensitive to the injury experienced by nonwhites. Unaware, we have adopted a worldview that takes for granted Black sacrifice.

Richard Delgado has suggested there is another way in which those of us who abhor racist speech but insist that it cannot be regulated may be, perhaps unwittingly, benefiting from the presence of "a certain amount of low-grade racism" in the environment:

> I believe that racist speech benefits powerful white-dominated institutions. The highly educated, refined persons who operate the University of Wisconsin, other universities, major corporations, would never, ever themselves utter a racial slur. That is the last thing they would do.
>
> Yet, they benefit, and on a subconscious level they know they benefit, from a certain amount of low-grade racism in the environment. If an occasional bigot or redneck calls one of us a nigger or spick one night late as we're on our way home from the library, that is all to the good. Please understand that I am not talking about the very heavy stuff—violence, beatings, bones in the nose. That brings out the TV cameras and the press and gives the university a black eye. I mean the daily, low-grade largely invisible stuff, the hassling, cruel remarks, and other things that would be covered by rules. This kind of behavior keeps non-white people on edge, a little off balance. We get these occasional reminders that we are different, and not really wanted. It prevents us from digging in too strongly, starting to think we could really belong here. It makes us a little introspective, a little unsure of ourselves; at the right low-grade level it prevents us from organizing on behalf of more important things. It assures that those of us of real spirit, real pride, just plain leave—all of which is quite a substantial benefit for the institution.[43]

"Which Side Are (We) On?"

However one comes out on the question of whether racist hate speech should be artificially distinguished from other fighting words and given first amendment protection, it is important to examine and take responsibility for the effects of how one participates in the debate. It is important to consider how our voice is heard. We must ask ourselves whether in our well-placed passion for preserving our first amendment freedoms we have been forceful enough in our personal condemnation of ideas we abhor, whether we have neglected our alliances with victims of the oppressive manifestations of the continuing dominance of these racist ideas within our communities and within ourselves.

At the core of the argument that we should resist all government regulation of speech is the ideal that the best cure for bad speech is good speech and that ideas that affirm equality and the worth of all individuals ultimately will prevail over racism, sexism, homophobia, and anti-Semitism because they are better ideas. Despite an optimism regarding the human capacity for good that can only be explained by faith, I am skeptical of ideals that provide the vehicle for oppressive ideology. I do not believe that truth will prevail in a rigged game or in a contest where the referees are on the payroll of the proponents of falsity. The argument that good speech ultimately drives out bad speech rests on a false premise unless those of us who fight racism are vigilant and unequivocal in that fight.

There is much about the way many civil libertarians have participated in the debate over the regulation of racist speech that causes the victims of that speech to wonder which side the civil libertarians are on. Those who raise their voices in protest against public sanctions against racist speech have not organized private protests against the voices of racism. It has been people of color, women, and gays who have held vigils at offending fraternity houses, staged candlelight marches and counterdemonstrations, and distributed flyers calling upon their classmates and colleagues to express their outrage at pervasive racism, sexism, and homophobia in their midst and to show their solidarity with its victims.

Traditional civil libertarians have been conspicuous largely in their absence from these group expressions of condemnation. Their failure to participate in this marketplace response to speech with more speech is often justified, paradoxically, as concern for the principle of free speech. When racial minorities or other victims of hate speech hold counterdemonstrations or engage in picketing, leafleting, heckling, or booing of racist speakers, civil libertarians often accuse them of private censorship, of seeking to silence opposing points of view. When both public and private responses to racist speech are rejected as contrary to the principle of free speech, it is no wonder that the victims of racism do not consider first amendment absolutists allies.

Blacks and other racial minorities also are made skeptical by the resistance encountered when we approach traditional civil liberties groups like the ACLU with suggestions that they at least reconsider the ways in which they engage in this complex debate concerning speech and equality. Traditional civil liberties lawyers typically have elected to stand by as universities respond to the outbreak of hate speech by adopting regulations that often are drafted with considerable attention to appeasing various, widely diverging political constituencies with only passing concern for either free speech or equality. Not surprisingly, these regulations are vague and overbroad. I believe that there is an element of unconscious collusion in the failure of universities, some with top-notch legal staffs and fine law schools, to draft narrow, carefully crafted regulations. For example, it is difficult to believe that anyone at the University of Michigan Law School was consulted in drafting the regulation that was struck down at that university.[44] It is almost as if the university administrators purposefully wrote an unconstitutional regulation so that they could say to the Black students, "We tried to help you, but the courts just won't let us do it." Such sloppy regulations provide easy prey for the white-hatted defenders of the first amendment faith who dutifully march into court to have them declared unconstitutional. Nor do some civil liberties lawyers stop there. They go on to point to the regulations' inadequacies as evidence that any regulation against racist speech may chill expression that should be protected.

Minority delegates to the 1989 ACLU biennial convention proposed a different approach. Their approach was to have the ACLU offer its expertise to schools and universities at the beginning of the legislative process instead of waiting until the end to attack a predictably unacceptable regulation. In the view of minority delegates, hearings should be held on university campuses where the incidence and nature of the injury of racist speech could be carefully documented and responses that were least restrictive of protected speech could be recommended. Such an approach would serve two important purposes. It would give civil libertarians an opportunity to influence the process from the outset, ensuring that the regulation reflected their constitutional concerns. It also would signal to racial minorities and other hate speech victims that the civil liberties community is aware of and concerned about issues of equality as well as free speech. But this approach to racist speech incidents was rejected at the national convention and has faced strong opposition when proposed to regional ACLU boards.

There is also a propensity among some civil libertarians to minimize the injury to the victims of racist speech and distance themselves from it by characterizing individual acts of racial harassment as aberrations, as isolated incidents in a community that is otherwise free of racism. When those persons who argue against the regulation of racist speech speak of "silencing a few creeps" or argue that "the harm that censors allege will result unless speech is forbidden rarely occurs," they demonstrate an unwillingness even to acknowledge the injury. Moreover, they disclaim any responsibility for its occurrence. A recent conversation with a colleague about an incident at Stanford exemplifies this phenomenon. Two white freshmen had defaced a poster bearing the likeness of Beethoven. They had colored the drawing of Beethoven brown, given it wild curly hair, big lips, and red eyes and posted it on the door of a Black student's dorm room in Ujamaa, the Black theme house. An investigation of the incident revealed that the two white students involved had been in an argument with the same Black student the night before. The white students contested the Black student's assertion that Beethoven was of African descent. It appeared that the Sambo-like defacement of the portrait was the white students' final rebuttal to the Black student's claim of familial relationship with the great composer—that this caricature was meant to ridicule the idea that such a genius could be Black— could be "Sambo."

My colleague shared my outrage at these students' behavior but went on to say that he thought that I had misinterpreted the import of the incident in viewing it as a manifestation of more widespread racism at Stanford. He was inclined to explain the students' behavior as that of two rather isolated, ignorant, misguided youths acting out against the dominant liberal culture. This hardly seemed an accurate description to me. The message conveyed by the defaced poster replicated, in a crude form, an argument that was being made by much of the Stanford faculty in the then-current debate over Stanford's course requirement in Western Civilization. The thrust of much of the argument for maintaining a Eurocentric curriculum that included no contributions of people of color was that there were no significant non-European contributions to be included. The students' defacement had added a graphic footnote to that argument. It seemed to me—contrary to my colleague's explanation of the students' behavior—that they were imitating their role models in the professorate, not rebelling against them.

In its most obvious manifestations, the recent outbreak of racism on our campuses provides an opportunity to examine the presence of less overt forms of racism within our educational institutions. But the debate that has followed these incidents has focused on the first amendment freedoms of the perpetrators rather than the university community's responsibility for creating an environment where such acts occur. The resurgence of flagrant racist acts has not occurred in a vacuum. It is evidence of more widespread resistance to change by those holding positions of dominance and privilege in institutions, which until recently were exclusively white. An atmosphere that engenders virulent racist speech is inseparable from practices that exclude minorities from university professorships and attitudes that devalue their contributions to the culture. Those who are marginalized in these institutions—by their token inclusion on faculties and administrations, by the exclusion of their cultures from core curricula, and by an ideology of diversity and multiculturalism that seems to require assimilation more than real change in the university—see their colleagues' attention to free speech as an avoidance of these larger issues of equality.

I believe that the speech/acts that "race" us must all be fought simultaneously, for they are mutually dependent parts of a whole. At Stanford I have responded to some of my colleagues who have urged that we turn our attention from the relatively trivial concern of racist speech to more important concerns like affirmative action by suggesting that we tie the two efforts together. Why not hold the university responsible for individual violations of a regulation against racial harassment, much as the employer is held responsible under Title VII of the Civil Rights Act for the harassing acts of its employees? Each time a violation of the regulation against racist speech occurs there would be a public intervention in the form of a hearing and a public announcement of the judicial body's findings of fact. Instead of the university punishing the individuals involved, an affirmative remedy or reparation would be made by the university to the injured class. The university might set aside a slot for a minority professor or fund an additional full scholarship for a minority student, or cancel classes for a day and hold a university-wide teach-in on racism. Such a proposal would directly address the institution's responsibility for maintaining a discrimination-free environment; it would have the symbolic value provided by a clear university position against certain forms of racist speech, and it would avoid first amendment problems by placing public sanctions on the institution rather than the individual speaker. If minority students knew that concrete institutional resources were being spent to change the atmosphere of racism on campus, they would be less concerned that individual racist speakers were escaping punishment. As things are, minority students hear the call for focus on racist attitudes and practices rather than on racist speech as "just a lot of cheap talk."

When the ACLU enters the debate by challenging the University of Michigan's efforts to provide a safe harbor for its Black, Latino, and Asian students (in a climate that a colleague of mine compared unfavorably with Mississippi in the 1960s), we should not be surprised that nonwhite students feel abandoned. When we respond to Stanford students' pleas for protection by accusing them of seeking to silence all who disagree with them, we paint the harassing bigot as a martyred defender of democracy. When we valorize bigotry, we must assume some responsibility for the assaultive acts of those emboldened by their newfound status as defenders of the faith. We must find ways to engage actively in speech and action that resists and counters the racist ideas the first amendment protects. If we fail in this duty, the victims of hate speech rightly assume we are aligned with their oppressors.

We must also begin to think creatively as lawyers. We must embark upon the development of a first amendment jurisprudence that is grounded in the reality of our history and contemporary experience, particularly the experiences of the victims of oppression. We must eschew abstractions of first amendment theory that proceed without attention to the dysfunction in the marketplace of ideas created by racism and unequal access to that market. We must think hard about how best to launch legal attacks against the most assaultive and indefensible forms of hate speech. Good lawyers can create exceptions and narrow interpretations limiting the harm of hate speech without opening the floodgates of censorship. We must weigh carefully and critically the competing constitutional values expressed in the first and fourteenth amendments.

A concrete step in this direction is the abandonment of overstated rhetorical and legal attacks on individuals who conscientiously seek to frame a public response to racism that preserves our first amendment liberties. I have ventured a second step in this chapter by suggesting that the regulation of certain face-to-face racial vilification on university campuses may be justified under current first amendment doctrine as an analogy to the protection of certain classes of captive audiences. Most important, we must continue this discussion. It must be a discussion in which the victims of racist speech are heard. We must be as attentive to the achievement of the constitutional ideal of equality as we are to the ideal of untrammeled expression. There can be no true free speech where there are still masters and slaves.

Epilogue

"Eeny, meeny, miney, mo."

It is recess time at the South Main Street School. It is 1952, and I am nine. Eddie Becker, Muck Makowski, John Thomas, Terry Flynn, Howie Martin, and I are standing in a circle, each with our right foot thrust forward. The toes of our black, high-top Keds sneakers touch, forming a tight hub of white rubber at the center, our skinny blue-jeaned legs extending like spokes from the hub. Heads bowed, we are intently watching Muck, who is hunkered down on one knee so that he can touch our toes as he calls out the rhyme. We are enthralled and entranced by the drama of this boyhood ritual, this customary pregame incantation. It is no less important than the game itself.

But my mind is not on the ritual. I have lost track of the count that will determine whose foot must be removed from the hub, who will no longer have a chance to be a captain in this game. I hardly feel Muck's index finger as it presses through the rubber to my toes. My mind is on the rhyme. I am the only Black boy in this circle of towheaded prepubescent males. Time stands still for me. My palms are sweaty and I feel a prickly heat at the back of my neck. I know that Muck will not say the word.

"Catch a tiger by the toe."

The heads stay down. No one looks at me. But I know that none of them is picturing the capture of a large striped animal. They are thinking of me, imagining my toe beneath the white rubber of my Keds sneaker—my toe attached to a large, dark, thick-lipped, burr-headed American fantasy/nightmare.

"If he hollers let him go."

Tigers don't holler. I wish I could right now.

My parents have told me to ignore this word that is ringing unuttered in my ears. "You must not allow those who speak it to make you feel small or ugly," they say. They are proud, Mississippi-bred Black professionals and longtime political activists. Oft-wounded veterans of the war against the racist speech/conduct of Jim Crow and his many relations, they have, on countless occasions, answered the bad speech/conduct of racism with the good speech/conduct of their lives—representing the race; being smarter, cleaner, and more morally upright than white folk to prove that Black folk are equal, are fully human—refuting the lies of the cultural myth that is American racism. "You must know that it is their smallness, their ugliness of which this word speaks," they say.

I am struggling to heed their words, to follow their example, but I feel powerless before this word and its minions. In a moment's time it has made me an other. In an instant it has rebuilt the wall between my friends' humanity and my own, the wall that I have so painstakingly disassembled.

I was good at games, not just a good athlete, but a strategist, a leader. I knew how to make my teammates feel good about themselves so that they played better. It just came naturally to me. I could choose up a team and make the members feel like family. When other folks felt good, I felt good too. Being good at games was the main tool I used to knock down the wall I'd found when I came to this white school in this white town. I looked forward to recess because that was when I could do the most damage to the wall. But now this rhyme, this word, had undone all my labors.

"Eeny, meeny, miney, mo."

I have no memory of who got to be captain that day or what game we played. I just wished Muck had used "One potato, two potato . . ." We always used that at home.

4

Words That Wound:
A Tort Action for Racial Insults,
Epithets, and Name Calling

Richard Delgado

In *Contreras v. Crown Zellerbach, Inc.*[1] the Washington Supreme Court held that a Mexican-American's allegations that fellow employees had subjected him to a campaign of racial abuse stated a claim against his employer for the tort of outrage. The plaintiff alleged that he had suffered "humiliation and embarrassment by reason of racial jokes, slurs and comments" and that the defendant's agents and employees had wrongfully accused him of stealing the employer's property, thereby preventing him from gaining employment and holding him up to public ridicule. Focusing upon the alleged racial abuse, the court declared that "racial epithets which were once part of common usage may not now be looked upon as 'mere insulting language.'"

Eleven months later, the United States Court of Appeals for the Seventh Circuit in *Collin v. Smith*[2] affirmed a federal district court's decision declaring unconstitutional certain ordinances of the Village of Skokie, Illinois, which had been drafted to block a demonstration by members of the National Socialist Party of America. The people of Skokie argued that the demonstration, together with the intended display of Nazi uniforms and swastikas, would inflict psychological trauma on its many Jewish citizens, some of whom had lived through the Holocaust. The court of appeals acknowledged that "many people would find [the] demonstration extremely mentally and emotionally disturbing." Mentioning *Contreras,* the court also noted that Illinois recognizes the "new tort" of intentional infliction of severe emotional distress, which might well include the uttering of racial slurs. Nevertheless, the threat of criminal penalties imposed by the ordinance was held impermissibly to abridge the plaintiffs' first amendment rights.

The concatenation of these two cases and the unsettled condition in which *Collin* leaves tort actions for racial speech suggest that reappraisal of these tort actions is in order. In this chapter I argue that an independent tort action for racial insults is both permissible and necessary. I will first examine the harms caused by racism and racial insults to the victims, to the perpetrators, and to society as a whole. I will then examine the various doctrines under which plaintiffs have brought lawsuits for racial insult, concluding that these doctrines fail to provide adequate protection against such language. I will next consider objections to an independent tort that are based on the difficulty of apportioning damages and on first amendment concerns. I will conclude with a brief sketch of the contours of the proposed cause of action.

Psychological, Sociological, and Political Effects of Racial Insults

U.S. society remains deeply afflicted by racism. Long before slavery became the mainstay of the plantation society of the antebellum South, European attitudes of racial superiority left their stamp on the developing culture of colonial America. Today, over a century after the abolition of slavery, many citizens suffer from discriminatory attitudes and practices, infecting our economic system, our cultural and political institutions, and the daily interactions of individuals. The idea that color is a badge of inferiority and a justification for the denial of opportunity and equal treatment is deeply ingrained.

The racial insult remains one of the most pervasive channels through which discriminatory attitudes are imparted. Such language injures the dignity and self-regard of the person to whom it is addressed, communicating the message that distinctions of race are distinctions of merit, dignity, status, and personhood. Not only does the listener learn and internalize the messages contained in racial insults, these messages also color our society's institutions and are transmitted to succeeding generations.

The Harms of Racism

The psychological harms caused by racial stigmatization are often much more severe than those created by other stereotyping actions. Unlike many characteristics upon which stigmatization may be based, membership in a racial minority can be considered neither self-induced nor alterable. Race-based stigmatization is, therefore, "one of the most fruitful causes of human misery. Poverty can be eliminated—but skin color cannot."[3] The plight of members of racial minorities may be compared with that of persons with physical disfigurements; the point has been made that a

> rebuff due to one's color puts [the victim] in very much the situation of the very ugly person or one suffering from a loathsome disease. The suffering . . . may

be aggravated by a consciousness of incurability and even blameworthiness, a self-reproaching which tends to leave the individual still more aware of his loneliness and unwantedness.[4]

The psychological impact of this type of verbal abuse has been described in various ways. The psychologist Kenneth Clark has observed, "Human beings . . . whose daily experience tells them that almost nowhere in society are they respected and granted the ordinary dignity and courtesy accorded to others will, as a matter of course, begin to doubt their own worth."[5] Minorities may come to believe the frequent accusations that they are lazy, ignorant, dirty, and superstitious."The accumulation of negative images . . . present[s] them with one massive and destructive choice: either to hate one's self, as culture so systematically demand[s], or to have no self at all, to be nothing."[6]

The psychological responses to such stigmatization consist of feelings of humiliation, isolation, and self-hatred. Consequently, it is neither unusual nor abnormal for stigmatized individuals to feel ambivalent about their self-worth and identity. This ambivalence arises from the stigmatized individual's awareness that others perceive him or her as falling short of societal standards, standards which the individual has adopted. Stigmatized individuals thus often are hypersensitive and anticipate pain at the prospect of contact with "normals."

It is no surprise, then, that racial stigmatization injures its victims' relationships with others. Racial tags deny minority individuals the possibility of neutral behavior in cross-racial contacts, thereby impairing the victims' capacity to form close interracial relationships. Moreover, the psychological responses of self-hatred and self-doubt unquestionably affect even the victims' relationships with members of their own group.

The psychological effects of racism may also result in mental illness and psychosomatic disease. The affected person may react by seeking escape through alcohol, drugs, or other kinds of antisocial behavior. The rates of narcotic use and admission to public psychiatric hospitals are much higher in minority communities than in society as a whole.

The achievement of high socioeconomic status does not diminish the psychological harms caused by prejudice. The effort to achieve success in business and managerial careers exacts a psychological toll even among exceptionally ambitious and upwardly mobile members of minority groups. Furthermore, those who succeed "do not enjoy the full benefits of their professional status within their organizations, because of inconsistent treatment by others resulting in continual psychological stress, strain, and frustration."[7] As a result, the incidence of severe psychological impairment caused by the environmental stress of prejudice and discrimination is not lower among minority group members of high socioeconomic status.

One of the most troubling effects of racial stigmatization is that it may affect parenting practices among minority group members, thereby perpetuating a tradition of failure. A recent study of minority mothers found that many denied the real significance of color in their lives, yet were morbidly sensitive to matters of race.[8] Some, as a defense against aggression, identified excessively with whites, accepting whiteness as superior. Most had negative expectations concerning life's chances. Such self-conscious, hypersensitive parents, preoccupied with the ambiguity of their own social position, are unlikely to raise confident, achievement-oriented, and emotionally stable children.

In addition to these long-term psychological harms of racial labeling, the stresses of racial abuse may have physical consequences. There is evidence that high blood pressure is associated with inhibited, constrained, or restricted anger, and not with genetic factors,[9] and that insults produce elevation in blood pressure. American Blacks have higher blood pressure levels and higher morbidity and mortality rates from hypertension, hypertensive disease, and stroke than do white counterparts. Further, there exists a strong correlation between degree of darkness of skin for Blacks and level of stress felt, a correlation that may be caused by the greater discrimination experienced by dark-skinned Blacks.

In addition to such emotional and physical consequences, racial stigmatization may damage a victim's pecuniary interests. The psychological injuries severely handicap the victim's pursuit of a career. The person who is timid, withdrawn, bitter, hypertense, or psychotic will almost certainly fare poorly in employment settings. An experiment in which Blacks and whites of similar aptitudes and capacities were put into a competitive situation found that the Blacks exhibited defeatism, halfhearted competitiveness, and "high expectancies of failure."[10] For many minority group members, the equalization of such quantifiable variables as salary and entry level would be an insufficient antidote to defeatist attitudes because the psychological price of attempting to compete is unaffordable; they are "programmed for failure." Additionally, career options for the victims of racism are closed off by institutional racism—the subtle and unconscious racism in schools, hiring decisions, and the other practices that determine the distribution of social benefits and responsibilities.

Unlike most of the actions for which tort law provides redress to the victim, racial labeling and racial insults directly harm the perpetrator. Bigotry harms the individuals who harbor it by reinforcing rigid thinking, thereby dulling their moral and social senses and possibly leading to a "mildly . . . paranoid" mentality.[11] There is little evidence that racial slurs serve as a "safety valve" for anxiety that would otherwise be expressed in violence.

Racism and racial stigmatization harm not only the victim and the perpetrator of individual racist acts but also society as a whole. Racism is a breach of the ideal of egalitarianism, that "all men are created equal" and each person is an equal moral agent, an ideal that is a cornerstone of the American moral and legal system. A society in which some members regularly are subjected to degradation because of their race hardly exemplifies this ideal. The failure of the legal system to redress the harms of racism and racial insults conveys to all the lesson that egalitarianism is not a fundamental principle; the law, through inaction, implicitly teaches that respect for individuals is of little importance. Moreover, unredressed breaches of the egalitarian ideal may demoralize all those who prefer to live in a truly equal society, making them unwilling participants in the perpetuation of racism and racial inequality.

To the extent that racism contributes to a class system, society has a para-mount interest in controlling or suppressing it. Racism injures the career prospects, social mobility, and interracial contacts of minority group mem-bers. This, in turn, impedes assimilation into the economic, social, and political mainstream of society and ensures that the victims of racism are seen and see themselves as outsiders. Indeed, racism can be seen as a force used by the majority to preserve an economically advantageous position for them-selves. But when individuals cannot or choose not to contribute their talents to a social system because they are demoralized or angry, or when they are actively prevented by racist institutions from fully contributing their talents, society as a whole loses.

Finally, and perhaps most disturbing, racism and racial labeling have an even greater impact on children than on adults. The effects of racial labeling are discernible early in life; at a young age, minority children exhibit self-hatred because of their color, and majority children learn to associate dark skin with undesirability and ugliness.[12] A few examples readily reveal the psychological damage of racial stigmatization on children. When presented with otherwise identical dolls, a Black child preferred the light-skinned one as a friend; she said that the dark-skinned one looked dirty or "not nice." Another child hated her skin color so intensely that she "vigorously lathered her arms and face with soap in an effort to wash away the dirt." She told the experimenter, "This morning I scrubbed and scrubbed and it came almost white." When asked about making a little girl out of clay, a Black child said that the group should use the white clay rather than the brown "because it will make a better girl." When asked to describe dolls that had the physical characteristics of Black people, young children chose adjectives such as "rough, funny, stupid, silly, smelly, stinky, dirty." Three-fourths of a group of four-year-old Black children favored white play companions; over half felt themselves inferior to whites. Some engaged in denial or falsification.

The Harms of Racial Insults

Immediate mental or emotional distress is the most obvious direct harm caused by a racial insult. Without question, mere words, whether racial or otherwise, can cause mental, emotional, or even physical harm to their target, especially if delivered in front of others or by a person in a position of authority. Racial insults, relying as they do on the unalterable fact of the victim's race and on the history of slavery and race discrimination in this country, have an even greater potential for harm than other insults.

Although the emotional damage caused is variable and depends on many factors, only one of which is the outrageousness of the insult, a racial insult is always a dignitary affront, a direct violation of the victim's right to be treated respectfully. Our moral and legal systems recognize the principle that individuals are entitled to treatment that does not denigrate their humanity through disrespect for their privacy or moral worth. This ideal has a high place in our traditions, finding expression in such principles as universal suffrage, the prohibition against cruel and unusual punishment, the protection of the fourth amendment against unreasonable searches, and the abolition of slavery. A racial insult is a serious transgression of this principle because it derogates by race, a characteristic central to one's self-image.

The wrong of this dignitary affront consists of the expression of a judgment that the victim of the racial slur is entitled to less than that to which all other citizens are entitled. Verbal tags provide a convenient means of categorization so that individuals may be treated as members of a class and assumed to share all the negative attitudes imputed to the class. Verbal tags thus make it easier for their users to justify their own superior position with respect to others. Racial insults also serve to keep the victim compliant. Such dignitary affronts are certainly no less harmful than others recognized by the law. Clearly, a society whose public law recognizes harm in the stigma of separate but equal schooling and the potential offensiveness of the required display of a state motto on automobile license plates, and whose private law sees actionable conduct in an unwanted kiss or the forcible removal of a person's hat, should also recognize the dignitary harm inflicted by a racial insult.

The need for legal redress for victims also is underscored by the fact that racial insults are intentional acts. The intentionality of racial insults is obvious: What other purpose could the insult serve? There can be little doubt that the dignitary affront of racial insults, except perhaps those that are overheard, is intentional and therefore most reprehensible. Most people today know that certain words are offensive and only calculated to wound. No other use remains for such words as "nigger," "wop," "spick," or "kike."

In addition to the harms of immediate emotional distress and infringement of dignity, racial insults inflict psychological harm upon the victim. Racial slurs may cause long-term emotional pain because they draw upon and intensify the effects of the stigmatization, labeling, and disrespectful treatment that the victim has previously undergone. Social scientists who have studied the effects of racism have found that speech that communicates low regard for an individual because of race "tends to create in the victim those very traits of 'inferiority' that it ascribes to him." Moreover, "even in the absence of more objective forms of discrimination—poor schools, menial jobs, and substandard housing—traditional stereotypes about the low ability and apathy of negroes and other minorities can operate as 'self-fulfilling prophecies.'"[13] These stereotypes, portraying members of a minority group as stupid, lazy, dirty, or untrustworthy, are often communicated either explicitly or implicitly through racial insults.

Because they constantly hear racist messages, minority children, not surprisingly, come to question their competence, intelligence, and worth. Much of the blame for the formation of these attitudes lies squarely on value-laden words, epithets, and racial names. These are the materials out of which each child "grows his own set of thoughts and feelings about race."[14] If the majority "defines them and their parents as no good, inadequate, dirty, incompetent, and stupid," the child will find it difficult not to accept those judgments.[15]

Victims of racial invective have few means of coping with the harms caused by the insults. Physical attacks are of course forbidden. "More speech" frequently is useless because it may provoke only further abuse or because the insulter is in a position of authority over the victim. Complaints to civil rights organizations also are meaningless unless they are followed by action to punish the offender. Adoption of a "they're well meaning but ignorant" attitude is another impotent response in light of the insidious psychological harms of racial slurs. When victimized by racist language, victims must be able to threaten and institute legal action, thereby relieving the sense of helplessness that leads to psychological harm and communicating to the perpetrator and to society that such abuse will not be tolerated either by its victims or by the courts.

Minority children possess even fewer means for coping with racial insults than do adults. "A child who finds himself rejected and attacked . . . is not likely to develop dignity and poise. . . . On the contrary he develops defenses. Like a dwarf in a world of menacing giants, he cannot fight on equal terms."[16] The child who is the victim of belittlement can react with only two unsuccessful strategies, hostility or passivity. Aggressive reactions can lead to consequences that reinforce the harm caused by the insults; children who behave aggressively in school are marked by their teachers as troublemakers, adding to the children's alienation and sense of rejection. Seemingly passive reactions have no better results; children who are passive toward their insulters turn the aggressive response on themselves; robbed of confidence and motivation, these children withdraw into moroseness, fantasy, and fear.

It is, of course, impossible to predict the degree of deterrence a cause of action in tort would create. But as Pier van den Berghe has written, "For most people living in racist societies racial prejudice is merely a special kind of convenient rationalization for rewarding behavior."[17] In other words, in racist societies "most members of the dominant group will exhibit both prejudice and discrimination,"[18] but only in conforming to social norms. Thus, "when social pressures and rewards for racism are absent, racial bigotry is more likely to be restricted to people for whom prejudice fulfills a psychological 'need.' In such a tolerant milieu prejudiced persons may even refrain from discriminating behavior to escape social disapproval."[19] Increasing the cost of racial insults thus would certainly decrease their frequency. Laws will never prevent violations altogether, but they will deter "whoever is deterrable."[20]

Because most citizens comply with legal rules, and this compliance in turn "reinforce[s] their own sentiments toward conformity,"[21] a tort action for racial insults would discourage such harmful activity through the teaching function of the law. The establishment of a legal norm "creates a public conscience and a standard for expected behavior that check overt signs of prejudice."[22] Legislation aims first at controlling only the acts that express undesired attitudes. But "when expression changes, thoughts too in the long run are likely to fall into line."[23] "Laws . . . restrain the middle range of mortals who need them as a mentor in molding their habits."[24] Thus, "if we create institutional arrangements in which exploitative behaviors are no longer reinforced, we will then succeed in changing attitudes" that underlie these behaviors.[25] Because racial attitudes of white Americans "typically follow rather than precede actual institutional [or legal] alteration,"[26] a tort for racial slurs is a promising vehicle for the eradication of racism.

Legal Protection from Racial Insults

The psychological, sociological, and political repercussions of the racial insult demonstrate the need for judicial relief. In the first part of this section I will examine the protection from racial insults afforded by current doctrine. The remainder of the section will be devoted to the objections likely to be raised against an independent tort action for racial slurs. In subsequent sections I will examine objections arising from tort law and first amendment objections.

Current Legal Protection from Racial Insults

Many of the arguments for a cause of action for racial insults are similar to the policies underlying causes of action for assault, battery, intentional infliction of emotional distress, defamation, and various statutory and constitutional causes of action, but each of these doctrines has limitations that render it an unreliable means of redress for the victims of racial insults.

Assault and Battery. In *Fisher v. Carrousel Motor Hotel, Inc.,*[27] the plaintiff, a mathematician attending a NASA convention in Texas, was accosted by a white restaurant employee while waiting in a cafeteria line. The employee snatched an empty plate from the plaintiff's hand and told him in a loud voice that he, a "Negro," could not eat in that cafeteria. The plaintiff did not allege that he was actually touched, or that he feared physical injury, but rather that he was "highly embarrassed and hurt" by the employee's actions in the presence of the plaintiff's associates. Although the jury awarded him $900, the trial judge denied any recovery. The Texas Court of Appeals affirmed, ruling that there had been neither a battery nor an assault and that under Texas law mental anguish without physical injury does not support a claim for damages in battery. The court reached this result even though the jury had found humiliation, indignity, and wanton disregard of the plaintiff's feelings.

The Texas Supreme Court reversed, finding that the plaintiff could recover under the rubric of battery because the waiter's seizure of the plate supplied the required offensive touching. The court further held that because battery is a tort designed to protect dignity as well as physical security, the plaintiff was not required to show physical harm in order to recover damages.

The holding in *Fisher* that the violent snatching of a plate from the plaintiff's hand constituted an offensive touching is not remarkable. But *Fisher* does indicate recognition by the Texas Supreme Court that racial insults and overt acts of discrimination can cause mental suffering and humiliation. Moreover, the facts of *Fisher* illustrate the inadequacies of the doctrines of assault and battery in protecting such a plaintiff. If the plate had not been snatched from the plaintiff's hand, but he had been insulted until he put down the plate and left, or before he picked up the plate, he could not have recovered in battery. And because the employee's words did not put the plaintiff in fear of physical injury or touching, the plaintiff could not have recovered in assault.

Intentional Infliction of Emotional Distress. Despite the ever-growing acceptance of intentional infliction of emotional distress as an independent tort, the perennial fear of a flood of fraudulent claims continues to mold the doctrine. The *Second Restatement of Torts,* for example, limits recovery to "severe emotional distress" caused by "extreme and outrageous conduct."[28] California permits recovery for physical injury to the plaintiff if the physical injury was foreseeable, but in the absence of physical harm, requires that the invasion of plaintiff's mental tranquility be "extreme and outrageous."[29] Utah requires that the distress be severe, that either the defendant have acted with the purpose of inflicting emotional distress or the distress be reasonably foreseeable, and that the defendant's actions be outrageous and intolerable.[30] In Texas, the emotional distress must be accompanied by physical injury.[31]

Yet, in addition to *Contreras,* courts on at least three occasions have upheld causes of action or verdicts for Black plaintiffs in cases that stemmed in large part from racial insults. Two of these cases are from California. In the first, *Alcorn v. Anbro Engineering, Inc.,*[32] a Black truck driver advised his supervisor that the supervisor had instructed another employee to violate union rules. The supervisor responded, "You goddam 'niggers' are not going to tell me about the rules. I don't want any 'niggers' working for me. I am getting rid of all the 'niggers' . . . you're fired." Alcorn alleged that he had been neither rude nor insubordinate and that the supervisor's conduct was intentional, malicious, and intended to cause humiliation and mental anguish. The court held these allegations sufficient to state a cause of action for "extreme and outrageous" intentional infliction of emotional distress. In so holding, the court emphasized the employee-employer relationship between the parties, the plaintiff's allegation of particular susceptibility to emotional distress, and developments in social consciousness that render the term "nigger" particularly offensive.

In the second case, *Agarwal v. Johnson,*[33] the plaintiff, a native of East India, sued his former employer and two of his former supervisors for repeated harassment. The plaintiff testified that on one occasion one of his supervisors had said to him, "You black nigger, member of an inferior race, get out and do it." The jury awarded the plaintiff general and punitive damages, and the state supreme court held that the evidence was sufficient to support the verdict for intentional infliction of emotional distress.

Because the question of whether the defendant's conduct is "extreme and outrageous" must be answered on a case-by-case basis and because the racial insults in these two cases were linked with other reprehensible conduct, including the unjustified termination of the plaintiff's employment, it is impossible to know whether the racial slurs were decisive factors in *Alcorn* and *Agarwal*. Courts always have been extremely reluctant to impose liability on the basis of words alone. The *Alcorn* court left open the question whether "mere insulting language, without more," could constitute "extreme outrage," and the *Agarwal* court stated that the plaintiff "presented substantial evidence that [one supervisor's] use of the racial epithet was outrageous."

In *Wiggs v. Courshon,*[34] the plaintiffs, a recent law graduate and his family, became engaged in an argument with a waitress serving them in the restaurant of the hotel in which they were staying while on vacation. The waitress said, "You can't talk to me like that, you black son-of-a-bitch. I will kill you." Later, she was overheard shouting repeatedly, "They are nothing but a bunch of niggers." The case was tried on the theory of assault, although the plaintiff also alleged mental anguish and emotional distress. At the close of the evidence, however, it was apparent that the plaintiffs were never reasonably in fear of physical injury. And under the controlling Florida law, plaintiffs may recover for intentional infliction of emotional distress only when that distress is "severe."

Nevertheless, the federal district court upheld the jury's verdict for the plaintiff on the basis of dictum in the controlling Florida Supreme Court decision, *Slocum v. Food Fair Stores of Florida, Inc.*[35] In that case, the plaintiff, a customer in a supermarket, asked a clerk the price of an item the clerk was marking. The clerk replied, "If you want to know the price, you'll have to find out the best way you can . . . you stink to me." The plaintiff sought to recover for her ensuing emotional distress and "heart attack and aggravation of pre-existing heart disease." The court held that these allegations did not state a cause of action because the "unwarranted intrusion [into the plaintiff's mental tranquility] must be calculated to cause 'severe emotional distress' to a person of ordinary sensibilities, in the absence of special knowledge or notice." Nevertheless, the court noted that a "broader rule has been developed" for "offense reasonably suffered by a patron from insult by a servant or employee of a carrier, hotel, theater, . . . [or] telegraph office." It was this dictum on which the *Wiggs* court grounded liability.

Wiggs exemplifies the shortcomings of the doctrine of intentional infliction of emotional distress as a means for redressing racial insults. The jury was eager to find for the plaintiffs, awarding them $25,000 in compensatory and punitive damages. But the judge was forced to ground liability on dictum that had never before been cited in the state and which had not been suggested to the court by either party. Most important, had the plaintiffs' dispute developed with another customer rather than an employee, no recovery would have been possible. The injury arguably is lesser when the perpetrator is simply another customer, but in *Wiggs* the plaintiffs' humiliation before the other diners would have been just as great and their vacation just as ruined.

Of course, the plaintiffs did win in *Contreras, Alcorn, Agarwal,* and *Wiggs.* But in at least two cases based substantially on racial insults, the plaintiffs lost because the defendants' actions were not sufficiently culpable. In *Irving v. J. L. Marsh, Inc.,*[36] the plaintiff, a Black architecture student, returned certain merchandise he had purchased to the defendant's store. In order to obtain a refund, he was required to sign a slip on the top of which defendant's employee had written, "Arrogant Nigger refuses exchange—says he doesn't like products." The court held that such conduct was not "sufficiently severe" for the plaintiff to recover. Similarly, in *Bradshaw v. Swagerty,*[37] the plaintiff, a young Black man, had been invited to the office of the defendant, a lawyer, to discuss accounts allegedly owed the defendant's client by the plaintiff and his brother. The conversation became heated, and the plaintiff alleged that the defendant called him "nigger," a claim that the defendant apparently did not deny. The court held that such epithets are "'mere insults' of the kind which must be tolerated in our roughened society" and affirmed summary judgment for the defendant.

The *Irving* court appeared sympathetic to the plaintiff, noting that "while the derogatory and highly offensive character of defendant's actions is not condoned by this court, the law, in its present state, does not permit recovery for the humiliation plaintiff was forced to endure." Arguably, then, the court's failure to impose liability resulted from the ever-present judicial fear of encouraging fraudulent claims and a flood of litigation. The court's reluctance to redress the plaintiff's injuries is symptomatic of the inadequacy of the tort for intentional infliction of emotional distress in such cases. One of the comments in the *Second Restatement of Torts* section on intentional infliction states in part, "The liability clearly does not extend to mere insults, indignities, threats, annoyances, petty oppressions, or other trivialities. . . . There must still be freedom to express an unflattering opinion, and some safety valve must be left through which irascible tempers may blow off relatively harmless steam."[38] What courts have thus far failed to recognize is that racial insults are in no way comparable to statements such as "You are a God damned woman and a God damned liar," which the *Restatement* gives as an example of a "mere insult." Racial insults are different qualitatively because they conjure up the entire history of racial discrimination in this country. No one would argue that slavery can be characterized as a "petty oppression" or lynch mobs as "mere annoyances," but thus far courts generally have not recognized the gravity of racial insults within the rubric of the tort of intentional infliction of emotional distress. Only an independent tort for racial insults can fully take into account the unique, powerfully evocative nature of racial insults and the insidious harms they inflict.

Defamation. In both *Irving* and *Bradshaw,* the plaintiffs also pled a cause of action in defamation, and both lost on that claim. In neither case did the plaintiff allege special damages, and thus both the *Irving* and *Bradshaw* courts ruled that the words alleged did not fit into any of the recognized categories of defamation per se. The *Bradshaw* court, however, did note, "The term 'nigger' is one of insult, abuse and belittlement harking back to slavery days. Its use is resented, and rightly so. It nevertheless is not within any category recognized as slanderous per se." Yet, interestingly, in at least three older cases, white plaintiffs were permitted to sue for defamation defendants who indicated that the plaintiffs were Black.[39]

It should not be surprising that defamation has failed to protect the victims of racial insults. "Defamation" is "an invasion of the interest in reputation and good name,"[40] although the law protects only victims of false defamatory statements. In contrast, the maker of a racial insult invades the victim's interest in emotional tranquility. A third party who learned that a person was the victim of a racial insult, but did not know the victim, would probably conclude that the victim is a member of a particular racial minority. But if this conclusion is true, the victim cannot recover because no falsehood has occurred. And whether or not the conclusion is true, it is not desirable that the law view membership in a racial minority as damaging to a person's reputation, even if some members of society consider it so.

Constitutional and Statutory Provisions. Victims of racial insults who have sued state officials under Section 1983, the federal civil rights statute,[41] have achieved differing results. In *Harris v. Harvey*,[42] for example, a Black police officer sued a white judge for a "racially motivated campaign to discredit and damage" the police officer and have him relieved of his job. As part of his extraordinary campaign, the judge had referred to the officer as a "black bastard." In affirming the jury's award of $260,000 in compensatory and punitive damages and the trial court's award of attorney's fees, the Seventh Circuit Court of Appeals held that "such an intentional tort inspired by racial animus and perpetrated under color of state law constitutes a denial of equal protection." The court also ruled that the judge's use of the power and prestige of his office brought his acts under color of law, even though the judge's campaign was not within the scope of his judicial duties, and thus the defense of judicial immunity was unavailable.

In contrast, in *Johnson v. Hackett*[43] a district court ruled that the complaint failed to state a claim under Section 1983. The plaintiff alleged that on a certain evening two uniformed police officers on patrol threatened to fight a group of Blacks and said that they would return later that evening. The officers did return, one asking, "Where are the night fighters?" the other asking, "What's a dead nigger anyway?" The next day, with the two officers again in uniform and on patrol, one of the officers called the plaintiff a "Chinese nigger." The plaintiff responded "with a similar expression, but without racial overtones." A third officer then asked the two officers if they had provoked the expression. After they replied that they had not, the third officer arrested the plaintiff for disorderly conduct.

The court held that there had been no infringement of the right to freedom from unlawful arrest and that the plaintiff's other alleged right, the "right to dignity," was not constitutionally protected. The court also reached the highly questionable conclusion that the two police officers had not acted under color of law because they were not authorized to call anyone insulting names. Reasoning that "the purely personal nature of the offer [to fight] is emphasized by the allegation that, before the challenge was issued, [the officer] removed his gun belt, laying aside, as it were, the symbol or 'pretense' of police authority," the court concluded, "It is the nature of the act performed, not the clothing of the actor or even the status of being on duty, or off duty, which determines whether the officer has acted under color of law."

The requirements of Section 1983—that the right infringed be granted by the U.S. Constitution or laws and that the official be acting under color of law—present formidable hurdles for victims of racial insults. The campaign of racial vilification in *Harris* was so extreme and unlikely to be repeated that one must conclude that the outcome in *Johnson,* not *Harris,* will emerge as the usual result.

If this is the case, it will be in sharp contrast to other areas in which the law increasingly is recognizing that the use of racial language by government officials is intolerable. The U.S. Supreme Court has found constitutional error in a contempt citation issued against a Black witness who refused to answer questions until the adverse attorney addressed her as "Miss Hamilton" rather than "Mary." And the Minnesota Supreme Court has held:

> We cannot regard use of the term "nigger" in reference to a black youth as anything but discrimination against that youth based on his race. . . . When a racial epithet is used to refer to a [black] person . . . an adverse distinction is implied between that person and other persons not of his race. The use of the term "nigger" has no place in the civil treatment of a citizen by a public official. We hold that use of this term by police officers coupled with all of the other uncontradicted acts described herein constituted discrimination because of race.[44]

Similarly, courts and administrative bodies have imposed duties to avoid racial language on prison officials, police officers, and school boards. In 1980 the San Francisco Civil Service Commission enacted a policy under which city officials and employees could be demoted, suspended, or dismissed for uttering racial slurs while on duty.[45] And in at least one case a jury has found government discrimination especially intolerable. In *Haddix v. Port of Seattle*,[46] a case brought under a state antidiscrimination statute against a government agency for four years of abusive treatment at the hands of a white foreman, the jury awarded the plaintiff $200,000, rather than the $145,000 the plaintiff had requested. One juror said, "We set the sum of $200,000 as a statement that race discrimination is wrong, and that the port is a public corporation and should be in the forefront of fighting discrimination."[47]

Despite this trend, victims of racial slurs have achieved mixed results when suing persons or entities other than government officials under various state or federal civil rights laws. Some plaintiffs have prevailed under state antidiscrimination statutes. For example, in *Imperial Diner, Inc. v. State Human Rights Appeal Board*,[48] a restaurant owner had told a waitress that she thought she was something special, "'Just like all the other f——ing Jewish broads around here.'" The owner repeatedly refused to apologize. The New York Court of Appeals affirmed the State Division of Human Rights ruling that the petitioner discriminated against the waitress by reviling her religion in a matter related to her working conditions and enforced the division's award of $500 to the waitress for "shock, humiliation, and outrage."

Other victims of racial slurs, however, have been less successful in their efforts to recover against private persons and entities under state and federal laws. An attempt to invoke federal civil rights laws to obtain relief failed in *Howard v. National Cash Register Co.*[49] In that case fellow employees had used the word "nigger" and other race-related language in plaintiff's presence. Although Title VII of the Civil Rights Act forbids an employer "to limit . . . his employees . . . in any way which would deprive or tend to deprive any individual of employment opportunities or otherwise adversely affect his status as employee, because of such individual's race,"[50] the court found that the racial abuse did not constitute employment discrimination. And in *Irving,* the court held that the plaintiff could not recover under an Illinois constitutional provision prohibiting "communications that portray criminality, depravity or lack of virtue in, or that incite violence, hatred, abuse or hostility toward, a person or group of persons by reason of or by reference to religious, racial, ethnic, national or regional affiliation,"[51] because that provision does not grant a private right of action.

Although it is correct to say, as did the Minnesota Supreme Court, that the use of a racial insult against a member of a minority group is race discrimination, apparently no court has found discrimination solely on the basis of a single racial insult. Courts appear unwilling to impose the vast liability and opprobrium that follow a finding of violation of federal and state antidiscrimination laws on the makers of racial insults. Recovery often is stymied further by the requirement incorporated in many of these statutes that there be some relationship between the parties, such as a contractual or employment relationship. And of course, it is reasonable to assume that there is substantial variation in the protection afforded by state antidiscrimination laws. Such problems would be eliminated by an independent tort for racial insults because it would protect all victims from racial insults regardless of the jurisdiction or the relationship between the parties.

Objections to a Tort for Racial Insults

Recognition of a tort for racial insults undoubtedly will face all the objections voiced whenever courts choose to protect a previously unrecognized interest—the difficulty of measuring and apportioning damages, the potential for fraudulent claims, and the prospect of a flood of litigation. Such objections, however, need not impede the recognition of a new tort. The now-recognized torts of invasion of privacy, intentional infliction of emotional distress, and compensation for prenatal injuries are illustrations of new causes of action that were fashioned to cope with substantial injuries that did not fit an existing category. As a leading torts commentator once observed, "The mere fact that the claim is novel will not of itself operate as a bar to the remedy."[52]

The Difficulty of Measuring Damages. One objection usually raised to torts that protect emotional well-being is that the intangible and highly subjective interests invaded are difficult to measure and prove. This objection has been rejected as applied to the tort of invasion of privacy, however, and is rapidly being surmounted in the case of intentional infliction of emotional distress. Behavior that injures a person's interest in repose and psychological well-being is now generally actionable despite the difficulties of measuring damages.

Moreover, a tort for racial insults contains an indisputable element of harm, the affront to dignity. The Harvard law professor Frank Michelman and others have argued that the intangible quality of novel interests should not, by itself, preclude valuing them for purposes of compensation.[53] Juries always can assign a value to such interests and their infringement. Alternatively, legislatures can set nominal damages to be recovered for the affront to dignity.

Of course, the law does not compensate for every inconvenience, bumped elbow, jostled shoulder or offended ear; against many of life's minor misfortunes a "toughening of the mental hide" is the best remedy.[54] Not every reference to a person's race or color is insulting, nor is every insult addressed to a minority person a racial insult. The cause of action suggested here is limited to language intended to demean by reference to race, which is understood as demeaning by reference to race, and which a reasonable person would recognize as a racial insult. The psychological or emotional harm alleged in such cases can be proved in the same manner as in other torts that protect psychological well-being. Expert testimony can be presented to substantiate the claim. Although such harms are to the mind and emotions, the harmful effects of racial speech have been amply studied and documented.

The Difficulty of Apportioning Damages.   A second potential objection to a tort for racial insults is the difficulty of apportioning damages. Of course, if proof of directly related emotional or psychological distress is produced, a defendant should be liable for this and any other reasonably foreseeable damages, such as medical expenses or loss of income. Absent these more tangible harms, juries should be free to set damages, within reasonable limits, to deter other wrongdoers. And because racial insults are almost always intentional and malicious, punitive damages may often be appropriate.

Even if the victim proves that the defendant's conduct caused the injury, the defendant may be able to show that the wrongful act, if committed in isolation, would have produced no harm. In other words, the defendant may assert that his or her conduct was only harmful because prior acts of racism rendered the plaintiff vulnerable to racial slurs. Such an assertion need not preclude liability, however, because tort law is reluctant to permit defendants to escape liability simply because other factors played a part in producing the plaintiff's injury.

Of the variety of approaches to apportioning damages, two would be relevant to a tort for racial insults. The first approach is to discount the harm to the victim attributable to the earlier actors and to require the present defendant to pay only for any additional harm. Prosser gives the example of a physician who negligently inflicts further injury on a patient injured by the defendant; although the defendant "may be" liable for the subsequent injury, the physician would never be liable for the acts of the defendant.[55] In the case of a racial insult, if the plaintiff's psychological and financial well-being has been damaged by earlier acts of racism, the present defendant would be required to account only for the incremental harm.

The second approach may be applied when the defendant has acted in concert with others to injure the victim. The theory of this approach is that the actors, "joint tortfeasors" under the common law, are each a part of a single enterprise, and thus the resulting harm is indivisible. This approach is relevant to a tort for racial insults because the maker of a racial slur necessarily calls upon the entire history of slavery and racial discrimination in this country to injure the victim. Thus the defendant is, in effect, a joint tort-feasor along with all others, past and present, who have perpetuated racism. Accordingly, the defendant should be liable for the full extent of the injury caused by the racial insult.

The real problem lurking within the issue of apportioning damages is the question of the plaintiff's susceptibility to racial insults. A defendant could argue that his or her own contribution to the injury was small compared to the overall effect of racism on the plaintiff or that the racial insult could have caused no damage because minority group members are or should be inured to such treatment. Further, the defendant could point to the circumstance that the "eggshell skull" rule, which states that a wrongdoer is liable for damages attributable to the plaintiff's peculiar susceptibility even if this susceptibility was not apparent to the wrongdoer, is not followed in intentional infliction of emotional distress cases.

The counterarguments, however, are more persuasive. That a defendant takes advantage of a plaintiff already harmed by earlier victimization makes the act more, not less, reprehensible; a contrary rule would imply that racial minorities are fair game for further abuse merely because previously they have been the object of similar abuse. Further, because a person's race is usually obvious, the maker of a racial insult is exploiting an apparent susceptibility rather than causing an unforeseeable injury, as in the eggshell skull cases. Such an exploitation creates liability even under the doctrine of intentional infliction of emotional distress, which recognizes that the "extreme and outrageous" character of the defendant's conduct may be supplied by the defendant's knowledge that the plaintiff is peculiarly susceptible to emotional distress.

Surprisingly, only two courts have addressed the problem of apportioning damages in racial insult cases. In *Alcorn,* the court stated in a footnote, "We cannot accept defendant's contention that plaintiff, as a truck driver, must have become accustomed to such abusive language. Plaintiff's own susceptibility to racial slurs and other discriminatory conduct is a question for the trier of fact, and cannot be determined on demurrer."[56] In *Contreras*, the court quoted this language with approval, adding, "It is for the trier of fact to determine, taking into account changing social conditions and plaintiff's own susceptibility, whether the particular conduct was sufficient to constitute extreme outrage."[57] That this issue has arisen in so few cases may suggest that once the liability of the defendants in racial insult cases is proved, the courts will not intervene to deny or reduce recovery because of the problem of apportioning damages.

Fraudulent Claims and a Flood of Litigation.   Because a tort for racial insults, like the other torts that protect psychological well-being, would present complex problems of proof of causation and of damages, it will face the objection that it would encourage fraudulent claims and generate a flood of litigation. In some jurisdictions, the fear of fraudulent claims is reflected in a rule that denies relief to plaintiffs who suffer no physical harm. Apparently, these jurisdictions believe that physical injuries are more easily proved and less easily feigned. Whatever its value in other contexts, this limitation is unnecessary in actions for racial insults. If racial invective is aimed at a victim, an infringement of the plaintiff's dignity, at the least, has occurred. Moreover, even if occasional plaintiffs win recoveries based on nonexistent damages, there is no reason to assume that these results would be erroneous more often than is the case in other types of civil litigation. At any rate, both correct and erroneous results would deter future offenses and thus protect the rights of others who cannot or will not seek redress.

The specter of a flood of litigation was also raised, and ultimately rejected, in connection with the torts of invasion of privacy and intentional infliction of emotional distress. Empirical studies show that the volume of litigation in response to the judicial recognition of new torts has not been overwhelming.[58] Moreover, the inconvenience and expense of a lawsuit will adequately deter frivolous or fraudulent claims. It is the role of courts to redress wrongs even at the risk of an increase in judicial business. A flood of litigation, therefore, would suggest that the courts were performing their function of placing the cost of the harm on the perpetrator. In addition, arguments based on a flood of litigation are most persuasive when adequate nonjudicial remedies are available. But because a tort for racial slurs implicates speech and thus requires balancing interests under the first amendment, it may not be possible to rely on nonjudicial forums.

Objections Based on the First Amendment

It is surprising, especially after *Collin*, that the question of whether racial insults are protected by the first amendment has not arisen in any case involving a racial insult. Until it does, the extent to which free speech considerations would shape the cause of action must remain an open question. No reported decision is on point; analysis can proceed only by examination of the nature of racial insults and the policies that underlie the first amendment.

Under first amendment doctrine, regulation of expressive activities is scrutinized more closely when directed at content of the speech rather than merely at the time, place, or manner of the speech in question. Because racial insults differ from ordinary, nonactionable insults precisely because they use racial terms for the purpose of demeaning the victim, a tort for racial insults will almost surely be seen as a regulation of content and thus be subject to the more exacting scrutiny afforded in such cases. But regardless of the standard applied, courts ultimately must balance the government's interest against that of the utterer of the infringed speech.

The Government Interests. The primary government interest served by a tort action for racial insults is the elimination of the harms of racism and racial insults discussed earlier. Not only the victim of a racial insult but also his or her children, future generations, and our entire society are harmed by racial invective and the tradition of racism that it furthers.

The government also has an interest in regulating the use of words harmful in themselves. In *Chaplinsky v. New Hampshire,*[59] the U.S. Supreme Court stated that words that "by their very utterance inflict injury or tend to incite an immediate breach of the peace" are not protected by the first amendment. Racial insults, and even some of the words that might be used in a racial insult, inflict injury by their very utterance. Words such as "nigger" and "spick" are badges of degradation even when used between friends; these words have no other connotation.

The Supreme Court also has recognized that in some contexts the government may restrict speech directed at a captive or unwilling audience. These cases have concerned speech both inside and outside the home. But in *Cohen v. California*[60] the Court overturned a conviction for wearing a jacket with the words "Fuck the Draft" written on it. In meeting the state's argument that the message was thrust upon unwilling listeners, the Court pointed out that viewers could simply avert their eyes.

Racial insults are easily distinguishable from the inscription in *Cohen.* One cannot avert one's ears from an insult. More important, a racial insult is directed at a particular victim; it is analogous to the statement "Fuck you," not the statement "Fuck the Draft." Finally, a racial insult, unlike the slogan in *Cohen,* is not political speech; its perpetrator intends not to discover truth or advocate social action, but to injure the victim.

The Free Speech Interests. Examination of the free speech values served by a racial insult is best undertaken within the framework of the categories outlined by Professor Thomas Irwin Emerson in his seminal article, "Toward a General Theory of the First Amendment."[61] He suggested four categories of values: individual self-fulfillment; ascertainment of the truth;

securing participation by the members of society in social and political decisionmaking; and maintaining a balance between stability and change.

Individual Self-Fulfillment. The values of individual self-fulfillment to
be furthered through free expression are based on the rights of individuals
to develop their full potential as members of the human community.
But bigotry, and thus the attendant expression of racism, stifles rather than
furthers the moral and social growth of the individual who harbors it.
In addition, a racial insult is only in small part an expression of self: It
is primarily an attempt to injure through the use of words. No one
would argue that the value of self-fulfillment is not limited by consideration
of the effects of one's means of expression on other members of society.
Although one may dress in Nazi uniforms and demonstrate before the city
hall in Skokie, Illinois, one may not paint swastikas on one's neighbors'
doors.

Ascertainment of the Truth. Emerson argued, "Through the acquisition
of new knowledge, the toleration of new ideas, the testing of opinion in
open competition, the discipline of rethinking its assumptions, a society will
be better able to reach common decisions that will meet the needs and aspi-
rations of its members."[62] This function of free speech, to achieve the best
decisions on matters of interest to all, has been extremely influential in first
amendment literature. Indeed, one theory of the first amendment is that the
amendment's protections extend only to speech that can be characterized as
"political."[63] In this respect most racial insults are distinguishable from the
expressions found protected in *Collin*. The plaintiff in *Collin*, the National
Socialist Party of America, was a political party whose race-related beliefs
were only a part of a set of ideals. But the characteristic most significant in
determining the value of racial insults is that they are not intended to inform
or convince the listener. Racial insults invite no discourse, and no speech in
response can cure the inflicted harm.

Racial insults may usefully be analogized to obscenity. Although the
government may regulate obscenity, it may not prohibit expression of the
view that obscenity should be protected or that, for example, adultery may
be proper behavior. Similarly, protecting members of racial minorities from
injury through racial insults and society itself from the accumulated harms of
racism is very different from prohibiting espousal of the view that race
discrimination is proper.

The reasons the Supreme Court articulated in explaining why obscenity
may be regulated are also instructive in analyzing racism and racial insults. In
Paris Adult Theatre I v. Slaton, the Court pointed to the "at least . . .
arguable correlation between obscene material and crime" and the "'right of
the Nation and of the States to maintain a decent society.'"[64] Racial insults,
through the racism and race discrimination they further, are severely at odds
with the goals of antidiscrimination laws and the commands of the thirteenth

amendment. A prohibition of such insults would surely further the government's interest in maintaining a "decent society."

Participation in Decisionmaking. In a democracy, as Emerson argued, all members of society must be permitted to voice their opinions so that the government's authority is derived in fact "from the consent of the governed."[65] Racial insults do not further this goal. On the contrary, they constitute "badges and incidents of slavery" and contribute to a stratified society in which political power is possessed by some and denied to others.

The Balance Between Stability and Change. Some of the many evils of the suppression of expression also are effects of racism and racial insults. Emerson mentioned the following arguments, among others, under the rubric of maintaining the balance between stability and change: Suppression of discussion substitutes force for logic; suppression of speech promotes institutional rigidity and inability to respond to changing circumstances; free expression leads those who lose public controversies to accept the result because they have had an opportunity to convert others to their opinion; and freedom of expression prevents violent upheavals by alerting the government to valid grievances.[66] But racism, in part through racial slurs, furthers all the evils caused by the suppression of speech. Racism dulls the moral and social senses of its perpetrators even as it disables its victims from fully participating in society and leaves unprejudiced members of society demoralized. Bigotry and systems of discrimination continue to exist for no reason other than that the prejudiced are in positions of power and authority. Institutions infected by these ills will be peopled by like-minded individuals and thus will be slow to respond to changing circumstances. Furthermore, racism excludes minorities from participating in the contemplation of public issues because their concerns are discounted by the majority and because they have been demoralized by repeated victimization. And it is painfully clear that this exclusion, not only from political discussion but also from the abundance of our country's wealth, is capable of leading to violent outbreaks.

Elements of the Cause of Action

In order to prevail in an action for a racial insult, the plaintiff should be required to prove that

> language was addressed to him or her by the defendant that was intended to demean through reference to race; that the plaintiff understood as intended to demean through reference to race; and that a reasonable person would recognize as a racial insult.

Thus, it would be expected that an epithet such as "You damn nigger" would almost always be found actionable, as it is highly insulting and highly racial. But an insult such as "You incompetent fool," directed at a Black person by a white, even in a context which made it highly insulting, would not be actionable because it lacks a racial component. "Boy," directed at a young Black male, might be actionable, depending on the speaker's intent, the hearer's understanding, and whether a reasonable person would consider it a racial insult in the particular context. "Hey, nigger," spoken affectionately between Black persons and used as a greeting, would not be actionable. An insult such as "You dumb honkey," directed at a white person, could be actionable under this formulation of the cause of action, but only in the unusual situations where the plaintiff would suffer harm from such an insult.

The plaintiff may be able to show aggravating circumstances, such as abuse of a position of power or authority, or knowledge of the victim's susceptibility to racial insults, that may render punitive damages appropriate. The common law defenses of privilege and mistake may be applicable, and retraction of the insult may mitigate damages.

Conclusion

I began this chapter by considering the serious harms inflicted by racism and racial insults and found that not only those to whom racial insults are addressed but also the perpetrators and society as a whole are victimized. Perhaps most disturbing, this review of the social science literature revealed that racism and racial insults influence the parenting practices of minority individuals and have a very great effect on children, thus perpetuating the harms of racism.

Next, I considered current legal protection from racial insults and determined that although plaintiffs have prevailed in actions based substantially on racial insults, the doctrines under which these plaintiffs sued have inherent limitations that ensure that many victims of racial insults will be unable to recover. Finally, objections to a independent tort for racial insults were considered, and it was concluded that these objections would not preclude the tort. I noted that the objections have not been squarely addressed in any case that has yet come before the courts, which may indicate that they have not been considered substantial by courts and practicing lawyers.

An independent tort for racial slurs would protect the interests of personality and equal citizenship that are part of our highest political traditions and moral values, thereby affirming the right of all citizens to lead their lives free from attacks on their dignity and psychological integrity. It is an avenue of redress that deserves explicit judicial recognition.

5

Beyond Racism and Misogyny:
Black Feminism and 2 Live Crew

Kimberlè Williams Crenshaw

Violence against women is a central issue in the feminist movement. As part of an overall strategy to change patterns of individual and institutional behavior to better women's lives, academics and activists have challenged the ways violence against women—primarily battering and rape—is perpetuated and condoned within our culture.

Much of this challenge has occurred within legal discourse because it is within the law that cultural attitudes are legitimized through organized state power. Feminists have struggled with some success to end the representation of battering and rape as a "private family matter" or as "errant sexuality" and make clear these are specific sites of gender subordination. These battles have taken place over issues such as mandatory arrest for batterers, the admissibility of a victim's sexual history in sexual assault cases, and the admissibility of psychological evidence, such as the battered women's syndrome in cases involving women who kill their batterers and rape trauma syndrome in sexual assault cases.

If recent events are indicative, the process may continue to bear some political fruit. The governors of Ohio and Maryland have commuted sentences of women convicted of murdering abusive husbands, and other states are considering similar actions. Moreover, legislation is pending before Congress that would make violence "motivated by gender" a civil rights violation.[1]

The emphasis on gender, however, tends to downplay the interaction of gender subordination with race and class. The attitude is largely consistent with doctrinal and political practices that construct racism and sexism as mutually exclusive. Given the assumption that all women stand to benefit from efforts to politicize violence against women, concerns about race may initially seem unnecessarily divisive. Indeed, it seems that what women have in common—the fact that they are primary targets of rape and battering—

not only outweighs the differences among them but may render bizarre the argument that race should play a significant role in the analysis of these issues.

Although racial issues are not explicitly a part of the politicization of gender, public controversies show that racial politics are often linked to gender violence in the way that the violence is experienced, how the interventions are shaped, or the manner in which the consequences are politicized and represented. The controversies over the Central Park jogger case, the 2 Live Crew case, the St. John's rape trial, and the perhaps lesser known issue of Shahrazad Ali's *The Blackman's Guide to the Blackwoman*,[2] all present issues of gender violence in which racial politics are deeply implicated but in ways that seem impossible to capture fully within existing frameworks that separate racial politics from gender politics. These separations are linked to the overall problem of the way racism and sexism are understood and how these understandings inform organizing around antiracism and feminism.

Reformist efforts to politicize these issues exclusively around gender are thus problematic both for women of color and for those engaged in feminist and antiracist politics generally. Discursive and political practices that separate race from gender and gender from race create complex problems of exclusion and distortion for women of color. Because monocausal frameworks are unlikely to provide a ready means for addressing the interplay of gender and race in cultural and political discourse on violence, it is necessary to recenter inquiries relating to violence against women from the vantage point of women of color. On the simplest level, an intersectional framework uncovers how the dual positioning of women of color as women and as members of a subordinated racial group bears upon violence committed against us. This dual positioning, or as some scholars have labeled it, double jeopardy, renders women of color vulnerable to the structural, political, and representational dynamics of both race and gender subordination. A framework attuned to the various ways that these dynamics intersect is a necessary prerequisite to exploring how this double vulnerability influences the way that violence against women of color is experienced and best addressed.

Second, an intersectional framework suggests ways in which political and representational practices relating to race and gender interrelate. This is relevant because the separate rhetorical strategies that characterize antiracist and feminist politics frequently intersect in ways that create new dilemmas for women of color. For example, political imperatives are frequently constructed from the perspectives of those who are dominant within either the race or gender categories in which women of color are situated, namely, white women or men of color. These priorities are grounded in efforts to address only racism or sexism—as those issues are understood by the dominant voices within these communities. Political strategies that challenge only certain subordinating practices while maintaining existing hierarchies not only marginalize those who are subject to multiple systems of subordination but also often result in oppositionalizing race and gender discourses. An intersectional critique is thus important in uncovering the ways in which the reformist politics of one discourse enforce subordinating aspects of another.

The observations that follow are meant to explore the ways in which intersections of race and gender bear upon depictions of violence against women, particularly women of color. My observations are also meant to explore the bearing of these intersections on the broader efforts to politicize violence against all women. I explicitly adopt a Black feminist stance in my attempt to survey violence against women of color. I do this with cognizance of several tensions that this perspective entails. The most significant one relates to the way in which feminism has been subject to the dual criticism of speaking *for* women of color through its invocation of the term "woman" even as it fails to examine differences and the problem of *excluding* women of color through grounding feminism on the experiences and interests of white women. I think it is important to name the perspective from which my own analysis is constructed, and that is as a Black feminist. I also think it is important to acknowledge that the materials upon which my analysis are based relate primarily to Black women. At the same time, I see my own work as part of a broader effort among feminist women of color to broaden feminism to include, among other factors, an analysis of race. Thus, I attempt to reach across racial differences to share my thinking and tentatively suggest ways in which the theory may apply to other women of color.

This chapter focuses on the problem of representational intersectionality. After a brief introduction to the theory of intersectionality, I will consider the ways in which media representations of women of color reinforce race and gender stereotypes. These stereotyped representations encourage and incite violence against us. But they do much more than that: They create a dominant narrative that forces actual women of color to the margins of the discourse and renders our own accounts of such victimization less credible. These media images define the spaces that women of color may occupy in dominant consciousness and problematize our efforts to construct a political practice and cultural critique that address the physical and material violence we experience.

This project is not oppositional to the overall effort to recode violence against women; rather, it is an attempt to broaden and strengthen the strategies available by exploring sites where race and gender converge to create the cultural and political grounding for gender violence. It is important also to ensure that these reform efforts do not reinforce racist sensibilities within the larger culture or ignore the need to challenge patriarchy within subcultures.

An Examination of Intersectionality

Intersectionality is a core concept both provisional and illustrative. Although the primary intersections that I explore here are between race and gender, the concept can and should be expanded by factoring in issues such as class, sexual orientation, age, and color. I conceive of intersectionality as a provisional concept that links contemporary politics with postmodern theory. In examining the intersections of race and gender, I engage the dominant assumptions that these are essentially separate; by tracing the categories to their intersections, I hope to suggest a methodology that will ultimately disrupt the tendencies to see race and gender as exclusive or separable categories. Intersectionality is thus in my view a transitional concept that links current concepts with their political consequences, and real world politics with postmodern insights. It can be replaced as our understanding of each category becomes more multidimensional. The basic function of intersectionality is to frame the following inquiry: How does the fact that women of color are simultaneously situated within at least two groups that are subjected to broad societal subordination bear upon problems traditionally viewed as monocausal—that is, gender discrimination or race discrimination. I believe three aspects of subordination are important: the structural dimensions of domination (structural intersectionality), the politics engendered by a particular system of domination (political intersectionality), and the representations of the dominated (representational intersectionality). These intersectionalities serve as metaphors for different ways in which women of color are situated between categories of race and gender when the two are regarded as mutually exclusive. I hope that a framework of intersection will facilitate a merging of race and gender discourses to uncover what lies hidden between them and to construct a better means of conceptualizing and politicizing violence against women of color. It is important to note that although I use these concepts in fairly specific ways, as metaphors their boundaries are neither finite nor rigid. Indeed, representational intersectionality is not only implicated in the political interactions of race and gender discourses, it can also be inclusive of these intersections. Moreover, political and representational intersectionality can also be included as aspects of structural intersectionality.

Structural Intersectionality

I use the term *structural intersectionality* to refer to the way in which women of color are situated within overlapping structures of subordination. Any particular disadvantage or disability is sometimes compounded by yet another disadvantage emanating from or reflecting the dynamics of a separate system of subordination. An analysis sensitive to structural intersections explores the lives of those at the bottom of multiple hierarchies to determine how the dynamics of each hierarchy exacerbates and compounds the consequences of another. The material consequences of the interaction of these multiple hierarchies in the lives of women of color is what I call structural intersectionality. Illustrations of structural intersectionality suggest that violence toward women usually occurs within a specific context that may vary considerably depending on the woman's race, class, and other social characteristics. These constraints can be better understood and addressed through a framework that links them to broader structures of subordination that intersect in fairly predictable ways.

One illustration of structural intersectionality is the way in which the burdens of illiteracy, responsibility for child care, poverty, lack of job skills, and pervasive discrimination weigh down many battered women of color who are trying to escape the cycle of abuse. That is, gender subordination—manifested in this case by battering—intersects with race and class disadvantage to shape and limit the opportunities for effective intervention.

Another illustration of structural intersectionality is the way in which battered immigrant women's vulnerabilities were particularly exploited by the Immigration Marriage Fraud Amendments of 1986,[3] which imposed a two-year wait for permanent-resident status on women who moved to this country to marry U.S. citizens or permanent residents, and which required that both spouses file the application for the wife's permanent-resident status. When faced with what they saw as a choice between securing protection from their batterers and securing protection from deportation, many women, not surprisingly, chose the latter. Even now that these provisions have been amended—primarily at the urging of immigration activists, not feminists, which is perhaps another testament to immigrant women's isolation under intersecting structures of subordination—immigrant women are still at risk. The amendment waives the two-year wait only for battered women who produce evidence of battering from authorities (such as police officers, psychologists, and school officials) to which immigrant women may have little access, and immigrant women may still lack the English-language skills, the privacy on the telephone, and the courage to transgress cultural barriers to ask for help. Further, women married to undocumented workers may suffer in silence for fear that the security of their entire family will be jeopardized should they seek help.

A final illustration of structural intersectionality is the way in which rape crisis centers in poor minority or immigrant communities must address rape survivors' homelessness, unemployment, poverty, hunger, distrust of law-enforcement officers, and perhaps their lack of English-language skills as well, often hindered by funding agency policies premised on the needs of middle-class white rape survivors.

Political Intersectionality

I use the term *political intersectionality* to refer to the different ways in which political and discursive practices relating to race and gender inter-relate, often erasing women of color. On some issues, the frameworks highlighting *race* and those highlighting *gender* are oppositional and potentially contradictory. These discourses are sometimes presented as either/or propositions, with the validity of each necessarily precluding the validity of the other. Manifestations of this oppositionality are found in antiracist and feminist rhetorical postures that implicitly or explicitly legitimize the dynamics of either racial or gender subordination. An extreme example is Shahrazad Ali's controversial book, *The Blackman's Guide to the Blackwoman* (1989), which blames the deteriorating conditions within the Black community on the failure of Black men to control their women. Ali recommends, among other practices, that Black men "discipline" disrespectful Black women by slapping them in the mouth—the mouth "because it is from that hole, in the lower part of her face, that all her rebellion culminates into words. Her unbridled tongue is a main reason she cannot get along with the Blackman."[4] More commonly, the need to protect the political or cultural integrity of the community is interpreted as precluding any public discussion of domestic violence. But suppressing information about domestic violence in the name of antiracism leaves unrevealed, and thus unaddressed in public discourse within our communities, the real terror in which many women of color live.

In other instances, women of color are erased when race and gender politics proceed on grounds that exclude or overlook the existence of women of color. Such an erasure took place in the rhetorical appeals made by sponsors of the Violence Against Women Act (1991).[5] White male senators eloquently urged passage of the bill because violence against women occurs everywhere, not just in the inner cities. That is, the senators attempted to persuade other whites that domestic violence is a problem because "these are *our* women being victimized." White women thus came into focus, and any authentic, sensitive attention to our images and our experience, which would probably have jeopardized the bill, faded into darkness.

But an erasure need not take place for us to be silenced. Tokenistic, objectifying, voyeuristic inclusion is at least as damaging as exclusion. We are as silenced when we appear in the margins as we are when we fail to appear at all.

Political intersectionality as it relates to violence against women of color reveals the ways in which politics centered around mutually exclusive notions of race and gender leave women of color without a political framework that will adequately contextualize the violence that occurs in our lives.

Representational Intersectionality

A final variant on the intersectional theme is *representational intersectionality,* referring to the way that race and gender images, readily available in our culture, converge to create unique and specific narratives deemed appropriate for women of color. Not surprisingly, the clearest convergences are those involving sexuality, perhaps because it is through sexuality that images of minorities and women are most sharply focused. Representational intersectionality is significant in exploring violence against women of color because it provides cues to the ways in which our experiences are weighed against counternarratives that cast doubt upon the validity and harm of such violence. I will analyze examples of representational intersectionality in images of violence against women—images that wound—in the next section.

Representational Intersectionality and Images That Wound

Representational intersectionality is manifest in the familiar images of women of color within popular culture. Here I examine the cultural images widely disseminated in the mainstream movies *Angel Heart, Colors, Year of the Dragon,* and *Tales from the Darkside: The Movie.* Next, I will discuss a video game called *General Custer's Revenge.* Finally, I will consider in more detail the debate surrounding the obscenity prosecution of 2 Live Crew's album *Nasty As They Wanna Be.*

Media images provide cues to understanding the ways in which women of color are imagined in our society. The images of Latina, African-American, Asian-American, and Native American women are constructed through combinations of readily available race and gender stereotypes. Because the stereotypes depicted in these presentations are quite familiar, collectively they form images of women of color that are specific and categorically unique.

Consider first the film *Colors. Colors* was a controversial film, but unfortunately none of the criticism addressed its portrayal of women. Yet the film was rife with familiar stereotypes. The obligatory sexual relationship in that movie occurred between a hot-headed white cop played by Sean Penn and a young Latina played by Maria Conchita Alonso, whom he encountered working at a fast-food stand. Their relationship and her characterization progressed as follows: In Scene 1, he flirts, she blushes. In Scene 2, she accompanies him to a family outing at his partner's home. In Scene 3, the crucial scene, he drops her off at her home. She almost maintains the "good girl" image that had been carefully constructed from the onset, but when she reaches her door, she reconsiders and turns back to invite him in for a night of sex. In subsequent scenes this nice, hardworking ethnic girl increasingly turns into a promiscuous schizophrenic Latina. In her final appearance, the transformation is complete. The scene begins with the young cop arriving to investigate a noisy house party. She is seen putting on her clothes in a bedroom from which a black man has departed. She wears a low-cut, loud dress and six-inch heels. She is very loud and brash now, laughingly tormenting the distraught and disappointed Sean Penn who upon seeing her, attempts to escape. She follows him and with her hands on her hips, demanding now in a very heavy and exaggerated accent: "Look at me. This is part of me too!"

This image of the good ethnic fiery Latina is contrasted with an image of

Black sexuality also constructed in *Colors*. In another scene, the police converge on a house to serve a warrant on a suspect named Rock-it. As they approach the house, the viewer hears a rhythmic squeaking and loud screams. The camera takes several seconds to track through the ramshackle house. There is little in the house except a stereo apparently playing the loud, pulsating music accenting the sound track. The camera turns a corner and finds a Black man and a Black woman on a bed, atop a single white sheet, so earnestly and frantically copulating that they are wholly oblivious to the several police officers surrounding them with guns drawn. When they finally became aware of the officers' presence, the man makes a sudden move and is shot several times in the back. As his lover screams hysterically, he gasps that he was simply reaching for his clothes.

In *Angel Heart*, the descent of an African-American woman into her own uncontrolled sexuality ends in tragic horror. Epiphany Proudfoot, played by Cosby-kid Lisa Bonet, is introduced washing her hair at a well. She appears at first the model of youth, reticent and exotic. Yet she's slightly fallen: She has a child whose father is unknown. Later we see her as a voodoo priestess dancing a blood-curdling ritual and collapsing in an uncontrolled sexual frenzy. The movie culminates in a vicious pornographic scene between Epiphany and Harry Angel (played by Mickey Rourke) that gives new meaning to the phrase "sex and violence." Sex—initiated by Epiphany— soon becomes gruesome as dripping water turns into blood, intercut with rivers of blood, deep thrusting, and screams of agony and horror. The visual narrative splits after this scene: Epiphany appears normal, singing a lovely lullaby and wistfully twisting her hair as she bathes, but later we discover that Epiphany is in fact dead. Her body sprawls across the bed, her legs spread open. A deep pool of blood surrounds her pelvic area. The movie's final scene plays out across her dead body. We discover the cause of her death when the Southern sheriff questioning Angel drawls, "Is that your gun up her snatch?" The horror is not yet complete, for we have still to discover that not only has Harry Angel killed his lover, but that this lover is actually his daughter. So this Cosby kid hits big time, being multiply victimized by incest, rape, and murder.

Perhaps it is happenstance that Lisa Bonet played Epiphany and that the imagery in this big-budget Hollywood film is so violent. Yet I wonder whether a Michelle Pfeiffer, a Kim Basinger, or even a Madonna would be asked to play such a role? I don't think so. The film, by relying on race-sex exoticism, works differently from the way it would with a white female. In fact, the presence of a woman of color often "makes" the story, as is still more clearly shown in an episode from *Tales from the Dark Side: The Movie*. The life of a young white artist is spared by a sixteen-foot talking gargoyle upon the artist's promise that he will never tell anyone that he has ever seen this gargoyle. Later that night he meets a Black woman, played here by Rae

Dawn Chong, whom he later marries and with whom he has two lovely children. With the support of his wife he becomes enormously successful, and they live a happy, fulfilled life. On their tenth anniversary, he decides to tell his wife this secret as a part of his expression of affection to her. Presenting her with a full-sized sculpture of the monster he tells her how his life was spared upon making a vow never to reveal that the monster exists. After he tells her the story, she becomes hysterical and, as "fate" would have it, begins to turn into the sixteen-foot gargoyle. Their two children emerge from the adjoining room as baby gargoyles. The wife disregards the artist's frantic efforts to profess his love for her, stating that she "loved him too but when the vow was broken their fate was sealed." She monstrously tears out his throat, gathers up the "children," and swoops through the ceiling. Here the drop-of-blood rule really works: The children, although half human, are little monsters, too. Can anyone doubt the message—white male miscegenators, beware! Exotica and danger go hand in hand.

Mickey Rourke, apparently bidding to be everybody's favorite racist/ sadomasochist/rapist/murderer, turns up again in *Year of the Dragon*. There he plays Captain Stanley White, a New York cop, who pursues a brash and independent Asian-American TV newscaster. He encounters her on the street, addresses her as a prostitute, taunts her with racist epithets (apparently learned from his days in Vietnam). After she invites him up to her apartment, he continues to assault her verbally, before physically doing so. He tells her that he hates everything about her, and then taking down his pants, he queries, "So why do I want to fuck you so badly?" The worst is yet to come: As our heroine rallies enough outrage to ask him to leave, he calls her a slant-eyed cunt. She slaps him once, pauses, and slaps again. He then grabs her, throws her down, rips off her clothes, and has forcible sex with her.

The next image comes not from a movie but from a video game, *General Custer's Revenge*. A Native American woman is tied to a pole. The player, General Custer, must traverse an obstacle course to get to the woman before getting shot. His saberlike penis leads him forward. The player wins when General Custer reaches the Native American woman and pounces on her. She "kicks up her legs in dubious delight" as he commits "what opponents call a rape and the manufacturer claims is a willing sex act." (A spokesman for the manufacturer commented, "There is a facsimile of intercourse. The woman is smiling.") Every stroke is a point. The motto: "When you score, you score."[6]

These four representations confirm both the feminist claim that women are legitimate targets for violence and the more specific observation that these targets are often represented with distinct racialized images. The Latina is two sided: She is both a sweet, hardworking ethnic and a loud, unscrupulous, racialized "other." The Black woman is wild and animal-like. In *Tales from the Darkside: The Movie*, she *is* an animal or, worse yet, a monster. The

Asian-American woman is passive. She can be verbally abused and physically assaulted, yet she still stands ready to please. The Native American woman is a savage. She has no honor and no integrity. She doesn't fight rape; in fact, being tied up and ravished makes her smile. She enjoys it.

In each of these cases the specific image is created within the intersection of race and gender. Although some claim that these images reflect certain attitudes that make women of color targets of sexual violence, the actual effect of images on behavior is still hotly contested. Whatever the relationship between imagery and actions is, it seems clear that these images do function to create counternarratives to the experiences of women of color that discredit our claims and render the violence that we experience unimportant. These images not only represent the devaluation of women of color, they may also reproduce it by providing viewers with both conscious and unconscious cues for interpreting the experiences of "others." Because both the actual experience of violence and the representations of those experiences constitute the "problem" of gender violence, feminists of color must address how race and gender intersect in popular discourse as well as in feminist and antiracist politics.

Addressing the Intersectionalities
in the 2 Live Crew Controversy

The different intersectionalities discussed above converge in my thinking on the controversy surrounding the obscenity prosecution of 2 Live Crew. The entire problem spurred by the prosecution of 2 Live Crew—the question of how to construct a Black feminist approach to the virulent misogyny in some rap music—has vexed me for some time, and as I suggested at the outset, prompted my attempt to construct a Black feminist understanding of gender violence.

The prosecution of 2 Live Crew began several months after the release of their *As Nasty As They Wanna Be* album. In the midst of the Mapplethorpe controversy and Tipper Gore's campaign to label offensive rock music, the Broward County sheriff, Nick Navarro, began investigating 2 Live Crew's *Nasty* recording at the behest of Jack Thompson, a fundamentalist attorney in Miami, Florida. The sheriff obtained an ex parte order declaring the recording obscene and presented copies of the order to local store owners, threatening them with arrest if they continued to sell the recording. 2 Live Crew filed a civil rights suit, and Sheriff Navarro sought a judicial determination labeling 2 Live Crew's *Nasty* recording obscene.[7] A federal court ruled that *Nasty* was obscene but granted 2 Live Crew permanent injunctive relief because the sheriff's action had subjected the recording to unconstitutional prior restraint. Two days after the judge declared the recording obscene, 2 Live Crew members were charged with giving an obscene performance at a club in Hollywood, Florida. Additionally, deputy sheriffs arrested a merchant who was selling copies of the *Nasty* recording. These events received national attention and the controversy quickly polarized into two camps. Writing in *Newsweek,* political columnist George Will staked out a case for the prosecution. He argued that *Nasty* was misogynistic filth. Will characterized the performance as a profoundly repugnant "combination of extreme infantilism and menace" that objectified Black women and represented them as suitable targets for sexual violence.[8]

The most prominent defense of 2 Live Crew was advanced by Professor Henry Louis Gates, Jr., an expert on African-American literature. In a *New York Times* op-ed piece and in testimony at the criminal trial, Gates contended that 2 Live Crew were literary geniuses operating within and inadvertently elaborating distinctively African-American forms of cultural expression.[9] Furthermore, the characteristic exaggeration featured in their lyrics served a political end: to explode popular racist stereotypes in a comically extreme form. Where Will saw a misogynistic assault on Black women by social degenerates, Gates found a form of "sexual carnivalesque" with the promise to free us from the pathologies of racism.

As a Black feminist, I felt the pull of each of these poles but not the compelling attractions of either. My immediate response to the criminal charges against 2 Live Crew was a feeling of being torn between standing with the brothers against a racist attack and standing against a frightening explosion of violent imagery directed to women like me. This reaction, I have come to believe, is a consequence of the location of Black women at the intersection of racial and sexual subordination. My experience of sharp internal division—if dissatisfaction with the idea that the "real issue" is race or gender is inertly juxtaposed—is characteristic of that location. Black feminism offers an intellectual and political response to that experience. Bringing together the different aspects of an otherwise divided sensibility, Black feminism argues that racial and sexual subordination are mutually reinforcing, that Black women are marginalized by a politics of race and of gender, and that a political response to each form of subordination must at the same time be a political response to both. When the controversy over 2 Live Crew is approached in light of such Black feminist sensibilities, an alternative to the dominant poles of the public debate emerges.

At the legal bottom line I agree with the supporters of 2 Live Crew that the obscenity prosecution was wrongheaded. But the reasons for my conclusion are not the same as the reasons generally offered in support of 2 Live Crew. I will come to those reasons shortly, but first I must emphasize that after listening to 2 Live Crew's lyrics along with those of other rap artists, my defense of 2 Live Crew, however careful, did not come easily.

On first hearing 2 Live Crew I was shocked; unlike Gates I did not "bust out laughing." One trivializes the issue by describing the images of women in *As Nasty As They Wanna Be* as simply "sexually explicit." We hear about cunts being fucked until backbones are cracked, asses being busted, dicks rammed down throats, and semen splattered across faces. Black women are cunts, bitches, and all-purpose "hos." Images of women in some of the other rap acts are even more horrifying: battering, rape, and rape-murder are often graphically detailed. Occasionally, we do hear Black women's voices, and those voices are sometimes oppositional. But the response to opposition typically returns to the central refrain: "Shut up, bitch. Suck my dick."

This is no mere braggadocio. Those of us who are concerned about the high rates of gender violence in our communities must be troubled by the possible connections between such images and violence against women. Children and teenagers are listening to this music, and I am concerned that the range of acceptable behavior is being broadened by the constant propagation of antiwomen imagery. I'm concerned, too, about young Black women who together with men are learning that their value lies between their legs. Unlike that of men, however, women's sexual value is portrayed as a depletable commodity: By expending it, boys become men and girls become whores.

Nasty is misogynist, and a Black feminist response to the case against 2 Live Crew should not depart from a full acknowledgement of that misogyny. But such a response must also consider whether an exclusive focus on issues of gender risks overlooking aspects of the prosecution of 2 Live Crew that raise serious questions of racism. And here is where the roots of my opposition to the obscenity prosecution lie.

An initial problem concerning the prosecution was its apparent selectivity. Even the most superficial comparison between 2 Live Crew and other mass-marketed sexual representations suggest the likelihood that race played some role in distinguishing 2 Live Crew as the first group to ever be prosecuted for obscenity in connection with a musical recording, and one of only a handful of recording groups or artists to be prosecuted for a live performance. Recent controversies about sexism, racism, and violence in popular culture point to a vast range of expression that might have provided targets for censorship, but that were left untouched. Madonna has acted out masturbation, portrayed the seduction of a priest, and insinuated group sex on stage. But she has never been prosecuted for obscenity. Whereas 2 Live Crew was performing in an adult's-only club in Hollywood, Florida, Andrew Dice Clay was performing nationwide on HBO. Well known for his racist "humor," Clay is also comparable to 2 Live Crew in sexual explicitness and misogyny. In his show, for example, Clay offers: "Eeny, meeny, miney, mo, suck my [expletive] and swallow slow," or "Lose the bra bitch." Moreover, graphic sexual images—many of them violent—were widely available in Broward County where 2 Live Crew's performance and trial took place.

According to the trial testimony of a vice detective named McCloud, "Nude dance shows and adult bookstores are scattered throughout the county where 2 Live Crew performed."[10] But again, no obscenity charges were leveled against the performers or producers of these representations.

In response to this charge of selectivity, it might be argued that the successful prosecution of 2 Live Crew demonstrates that its lyrics were uniquely obscene. In a sense, this argument runs, the proof is in the prosecution—if they were not uniquely obscene, they would have been acquitted. However, the elements of 2 Live Crew's performance that contributed initially to their selective arrest continued to play out as the court applied the obscenity standard to the recording. To clarify this argument, we need to consider the technical use of "obscenity" as a legal term of art. For the purposes of legal argument, the Supreme Court in the 1973 case of *Miller v. California* held that a work is obscene if and only if it meets each of three conditions: (1) "the average person, applying community standards, would find that the work, taken as a whole, appeals to the prurient interest"; (2) "the work depicts or describes, in a patently offensive way, sexual conduct specifically defined by the applicable state law"; and (3) "the work, take as a whole, lacks serious literary, artistic, political, or scientific value."[11] The Court held that it is consistent with first amendment guarantees of freedom of expression for states to subject work that meets each of the three prongs of the *Miller* test to very restrictive regulations.

Focusing first on the prurient interest prong of the *Miller* test, we might wonder how 2 Live Crew could have been seen as uniquely obscene by the lights of the "community standards" of Broward County. After all, as Detective McCloud put it, "Patrons [of clubs in Broward] can see women dancing with at least their breasts exposed" and bookstore patrons can "view and purchase films and magazines that depict vaginal, oral and anal sex, homosexual sex and group sex."[12] In arriving at its finding of obscenity, the court placed little weight on the available range of films, magazines, and live shows as evidence of the community's sensibilities. Instead, the court apparently accepted the sheriff's testimony that the decision to single out *Nasty* was based on the number of complaints against 2 Live Crew, "communicated by telephone calls, anonymous messages, or letters to the police."[13]

Evidence of this popular outcry was never substantiated. But even if it were, the case for selectivity would remain. The history of social repression of Black male sexuality is long, often violent, and all too familiar. Negative reactions against the sexual conduct of Black males have traditionally had racist overtones, especially where that conduct threatens to "cross over" into the mainstream community. So even if the decision to prosecute did reflect a widespread community perception of the purely prurient character of 2 Live Crew's music, that perception itself might reflect an established pattern of vigilante attitudes directed toward the sexual expression of Black males. In short, the appeal to community standards does not undercut a concern about racism; rather, it underscores that concern.

A second troubling dimension of the case against 2 Live Crew was the court's apparent disregard for the culturally rooted aspects of 2 Live Crew's music. Such disregard was essential to a finding of obscenity given the third prong of the *Miller* test, requiring that obscene material lack any literary, artistic, or political value. 2 Live Crew argued that this test was not met because the recording exemplified such African-American cultural modes as "playing the dozens," "call and response," and "signifying." As a storehouse of such cultural modes, it could not be said that *Nasty* could be described as completely devoid of literary or artistic value. In each case the court denied the group's claim of cultural specificity by recharacterizing those modes claimed to be African American in more generic terms. For example, the court reasoned that playing the dozens is "commonly seen in adolescents, especially boys, of all ages." "Boasting," the court observed, appears to be "part of the universal human condition." And the court noted that the cultural origins of one song featuring call and response—a song about fellatio in which competing groups chanted "less filling" and "tastes great"—were to be found in a Miller beer commercial, not in African-American cultural tradition. The possibility that the Miller beer commercial may have itself evolved from an African-American cultural tradition was lost on the court.

In disregarding this testimony the court denied the artistic value in the form and style of *Nasty* and, by implication, rap music more generally. This disturbing dismissal of the cultural attributes of rap and the effort to universalize African-American modes of expression flattens cultural differences. The court's analysis here manifests in the law a frequently encountered strategy of cultural appropriation. African-American contributions accepted by be mainstream culture are considered simply "American" or found to be "universal." Other modes associated with African-American culture that resist absorption and remain distinctive are neglected or dismissed as "deviant."

An additional concern has as much to do with the obscenity doctrine itself as with the court's application of it in this case. The case illustrates the ways in which obscenity doctrine asks the wrong questions with respect to sexual violence and facilitates the wrong conclusions with respect to racially selective enforcement. As I mentioned earlier, obscenity requires a determination that the material be intended to appeal to the prurient interest. In making this determination, the court rejected the relevance of 2 Live Crew's admitted motives—both their larger motive of making money and their secondary motive of doing so through the marketing of outrageous sexual humor. Although the prurient interest requirement eludes precise definition—recall Potter Stewart's infamous declaration that "I know it when I see it"—it seems clear that it must appeal in some immediate way to sexual desire. It would be difficult to say definitively what does or does not constitute an appeal to this prurient interest, but one can surmise that the twenty-five-cent peep shows that are standard fare in Broward County rank considerably higher on this scale than the sexual tall tales told by 2 Live Crew.

2 Live Crew is thus one of the lesser candidates in the prurient interest sweepstakes mandated by the obscenity standard, and it is also a lesser contender by another measure that lies explicitly outside the obscenity doctrine: violence. Compared to groups such as N.W.A., Too Short, Ice Cube, and the Geto Boys, 2 Live Crew's misogynistic hyperbole sounds minor league. Sometimes called gangsta' rap, the lyrics offered by these other groups celebrate violent assault, rape, rape-murder, and mutilation. Had these other groups been targeted rather than the comparatively less offensive 2 Live Crew, they may have been more successful in defeating the prosecution. The graphic violence in their representations militates against a finding of obscenity by suggesting an intent to appeal not to prurient interests but instead to the fantasy of the social outlaw. Indeed, these appeals might even be read as political. Against the historical backdrop in which the image of the Black male as social outlaw is a prominent theme, gangsta' rap might be read as a rejection of a conciliatory stance aimed at undermining fear through reassurance in favor of a more subversive form of opposition that attempts to challenge the rules precisely by becoming the very social outlaw that society has proscribed. Thus, so long as obscenity remains preoccupied with finding prurient interests and violent imagery is seen as distinct from sexuality, obscenity doctrine is ineffectual against more violent rappers.

Yet even this somewhat formal dichotomy between sex, which obscenity is concerned about, and violence, which lies beyond its purview, may provide little solace to the entire spectrum of rappers ranging from the Geto Boys to 2 Live Crew. Given the historical linkages between Black male sexuality and violence, the two are likely to be directly linked in the prurient interest inquiry, even if subconsciously. In fact, it may have been the background images of Black male sexual violence that rendered 2 Live Crew an acceptable target for obscenity in a lineup that included many stronger contenders.

My point here is not to suggest that the distinction between sex and violence should be maintained in obscenity, nor more specifically, that the more violent rappers ought to be protected. To the contrary, these groups trouble me much more than 2 Live Crew. My point instead is to suggest that obscenity doctrine does nothing to protect the interests of those who are most directly implicated in such rap—Black women. On a formal level, obscenity separates out sexuality and violence, thus shielding the more violently misogynist groups from prosecution. Yet the historical linkages between images of Black male sexuality and violence simultaneously single out lightweight rappers for prosecution among all other purveyors of explicit sexual imagery. Neither course furthers Black women's simultaneous interests in opposing racism and misogyny.

Although Black women's interests were quite obviously irrelevant in this obscenity judgment, their bodies figured prominently in the public case supporting the prosecution. George Will's *Newsweek* essay provides a striking example of how Black women's bodies were appropriated and deployed in the broader attack against 2 Live Crew. In "America's Slide into the Sewers," Will told us, "America today is capable of terrific intolerance about smoking, or toxic waste that threatens trout. But only a deeply confused society is more concerned about protecting lungs than minds, trout than black women. We legislate against smoking in restaurants; singing 'Me So Horny' is a constitutional right. Secondary smoke is carcinogenic; celebration of torn vaginas is 'mere words.'"[14]

Notwithstanding these expressions of concern about Black women, Will's real worry is suggested by his repeated references to the Central Park jogger. He writes, "Her face was so disfigured a friend took 15 minutes to identify her. 'I recognized her ring.' Do you recognize the relevance of 2 Live Crew?" Although the connection between the threat of 2 Live Crew and the image of the Black male rapist was suggested subtly in the public debate, it is manifest throughout Will's discussion and in fact bids to be its central theme. "Fact: Some members of a particular age and societal cohort—the one making 2 Live Crew rich—stomped and raped the jogger to the razor edge of death, for the fun of it." Will directly indicts 2 Live Crew in the Central Park jogger rape through a fictional dialogue between himself and the defendants. Responding to one defendant's alleged confession that the rape was fun, Will asks: "Where can you get the idea that sexual violence against women is fun? From a music store, through Walkman earphones, from boom boxes blaring forth the rap lyrics of 2 Live Crew"; because the rapists were young Black males and *Nasty* presents Black men celebrating sexual violence, surely 2 Live Crew was responsible. Apparently, the vast American industry that markets misogynistic representation in every conceivable way is irrelevant to understanding this particular incident of sexual violence.

Will invokes Black women—twice—as victims of this music. But if he were really concerned with the threat to Black women, why does the Central Park jogger figure so prominently in his argument? Why not the Black woman from Brooklyn who, within weeks of the Central Park assault, was gang-raped and then thrown down an air shaft? What about the twenty-eight other women—mostly women of color—who were raped in New York City the same week the Central Park jogger was raped? Rather than being centered in Will's display of concern, Black women appear to function as stand-ins for white women. The focus on sexual violence played out on Black women's bodies seems to reflect concerns about the threat to Black male violence against the strategy of the prosecutor in Richard Wright's novel *Native Son.*[15] Bigger Thomas, the Black male protagonist, is on trial for killing Mary Dalton, a white woman. Because Bigger burned her body, however, it cannot be established whether Mary was raped. So the prosecutor brings in the body of Bessie, a Black woman raped by Bigger and left to die, to establish that Bigger had raped Mary.

Further evidence that Will's concern about sexual imagery and rape is grounded in familiar narratives of Black sexual violence and white victimhood is suggested by his nearly apoplectic reaction to similar attempts to regulate racist speech. In his assault on 2 Live Crew, Will decries liberal tolerance for lyrics that "desensitize" our society and that will certainly have "behavioral consequences." Proponents of campus speech regulations have made arguments that racist speech facilitates racist violence in much the same way that Will links rap to sexual violence. Yet Will has excoriated such proponents.

Despite his anguish that sexual lyrics "coarsen" our society and facilitate a "slide into the sewer," in Will's view,[16] racist speech is situated on a much higher plane. Apparently, the "social cohort" that is most likely to engage in racial violence—young white men—has sense enough to distinguish ideas from action whereas the "social cohort" that identifies with 2 Live Crew is made up of mindless brutes who will take rap as literal encouragement to rape. Will's position on racist speech not only indicates how readily manipulable the link between expression and action is, but suggests further reasons why his invocation of Black women seems so disingenuous. One can't help but wonder why Will is so outraged about attacks on Black women's vaginal walls and not concerned about attacks on our skin.

These concerns about selectivity in prosecution, about the denial of cultural specificity, and about the manipulation of Black women's bodies convince me that race played a significant if not determining role in the shaping of the case against 2 Live Crew. While using antisexist rhetoric to suggest a concern for women, the attack simultaneously endorsed traditional readings of Black male sexuality. The fact that most sexual violence involves intraracial assault fades to the background as the Black male is represented as the agent of sexual violence and the white community is represented as his victim. The subtext of the 2 Live Crew prosecution thus becomes a re-reading of the sexualized racial politics of the past.

Although concerns about racism fuel my opposition to the obscenity prosecution, I am also troubled by the uncritical support for and indeed celebration of 2 Live Crew by other opponents of that prosecution. If the rhetoric of antisexism provided an occasion for racism, so too, the rhetoric of antiracism provided an occasion for defending the misogyny of Black male rappers.

The defense of 2 Live Crew took two forms, one political and one cultural, both of which were advanced most prominently by Henry Louis Gates, Jr. The political argument was that 2 Live Crew represents an attack against Black sexual stereotypes. The strategy of the attack is, in Gates's words, to "exaggerate [the] stereotypes" and thereby "to show how ridiculous the portrayals are."[17] For the strategy to succeed, it must of course highlight the sexism, misogyny, and violence stereotypically associated with Black male sexuality. But far from embracing that popular mythology, the idea is to fight the racism of those who accept it. Thus, the argument goes, 2 Live Crew and other rap groups are simply pushing white society's buttons to ridicule its dominant sexual images.

I agree with Gates that the reactions by Will and others to 2 Live Crew confirm that the stereotypes still exist and still evoke basic fears. But even if I were to agree that 2 Live Crew intended to explode these mythic fears, I still would argue that its strategy was wholly misguided. These fears are too active and African Americans are too closely associated with them not to be burned when the myths are exploded. More fundamentally, however, I am deeply skeptical about the claim that the Crew was engaged—either in intent or effects—in a postmodern guerrilla war against racist stereotypes.

Gates argues that when one listens to 2 Live Crew, the ridiculous stories and the hyperbole make the listener "bust out laughing." Apparently, the fact that Gates and many other people react with laughter confirms and satisfies the Crew's objective of ridiculing the stereotypes. The fact that the Crew is often successful in achieving laughter neither substantiates Gates's reading, nor forecloses serious critique of its subordinating dimensions.

In disagreeing with Gates, I do not mean to suggest that 2 Live Crew's lyrics are to be taken literally. But rather than exploding stereotypes as Gates suggests, I believe that the group simply uses readily available sexual images in trying to be funny. Trading in racial stereotypes and sexual hyperbole are well-rehearsed strategies for achieving laughter; the most extreme representations often do more to reinforce and entrench the image than to explode it. 2 Live Crew departs from this tradition only in its attempt to up the ante through more outrageous boasts and more explicit manifestations of misogyny.

The acknowledgement, however, that the Crew was simply trying to be funny should not be interpreted as constituting a defense against its misogyny. Neither the intent to be funny nor Gates's loftier explanations negate the subordinating qualities of such humor. An examination of the parallel arguments in the context of racist humor suggests why neither claim functions as a persuasive defense for 2 Live Crew.

Gates's use of laughter as a defensive maneuver in the attack on 2 Live Crew recalls similar strategies in defense of racist humor. Racist humor has sometimes been defended as antiracist—an effort to poke fun at or to show the ridiculousness of racism. More simply, racist humor has often been excused as just joking; even racially motivated assaults are often defended as simple pranks. Thus, the racism and sexism of Andrew Dice Clay could be defended either as an attempt to explode the stereotypes of white racists or more simply as simple humor not meant to be taken seriously. Implicit in these defenses is the assumption that racist representations are injurious only if they are devoid of any other objective or are meant to be taken literally. Although these arguments are familiar within the Black community, I think it is highly unlikely that they would be viewed as a persuasive defense of Andrew Dice Clay. Indeed, the historical and ongoing criticism of such humor suggests widespread rejection of such disclaimers. Operating instead under a premise that humor can be nonliteral, perhaps even well intended, but racist nonetheless, African Americans have protested such humor. This practice of opposition suggests a general recognition within the Black community that "mere humor" is not inconsistent with subordination. The question of what people find humorous is of course a complicated one that includes considerations of aggression, reinforcement of group boundaries, projection, and other issues. The claim of intending only a joke may be true, but representations function as humor within a specific social context and frequently reinforce patterns of social power. Even though racial humor may sometimes be intended to ridicule racism, the close relationship between the stereotypes and the prevailing images of marginalized people as well as a presumed connection between the humorist and the dominant audience complicates this strategy. Clearly, racial humor does not always undermine the racism of the character speaking nor indict the wider society in which the jokes have meaning. The endearment of Archie Bunker seems to suggest at least this much.

Thus, in the context of racist humor, neither the fact that people actually laughed at racist humor nor the usual disclaimer of intent have functioned to preclude incisive and often quite angry criticism of such humor within the African-American community. Although a similar set of arguments could be offered in the context of sexist humor, images marketed by 2 Live Crew were not condemned, but as Gates illustrates, defended, often with great commitment and skill. Clearly, the fact that the Crew is Black, as are the women it objectifies, shaped this response. There is of course an ongoing issue of how one's positioning vis-à-vis a targeted group colors the way the group interprets a potentially derisive stereotype or gesture. Had 2 Live Crew been whites in blackface, for example, all of the readings would have been different. Although the question of whether one can defend the broader license given to Black comedians to market stereotypical images is an interesting one, it is not the issue here. 2 Live Crew cannot claim an in-group privilege to perpetuate misogynistic humor against Black women. Its members are not Black women, and more important, they enjoy a power relationship over them.

Sexual humor in which women are objectified as packages of bodily parts to serve whatever male-bonding/male-competition the speakers please subordinates women in much the same way that racist humor subordinates African Americans. That these are "just jokes" and are not taken as literal claims does little to blunt their demeaning quality—nor, for that matter, does it help that the jokes are told within a tradition of intragroup humor.

Gates offered a second, cultural defense of 2 Live Crew: the idea that *Nasty* is in line with distinctively African-American traditions of culture. It is true that the dozens and other forms of verbal boasting have been practiced within the Black community for some time. It is true as well that raunchy jokes, insinuations, and boasts of sexual prowess were not meant to be taken literally. Nor, however, were they meant to disrupt conventional myths about Black sexuality. They were meant simply to be laughed at and perhaps to gain respect for the speaker's word wizardry.

Ultimately, however, little turns on whether the "wordplay" performed by 2 Live Crew is a postmodern challenge to racist sexual mythology or simply an internal group practice that has crossed over into mainstream U.S. society. Both versions of the defense are problematic because both call on Black women to accept misogyny and its attendant disrespect in the service of some broader group objective. Whereas one version argues that accepting misogyny is necessary to antiracist politics, the other argues that it is necessary to maintain the cultural integrity of the community. Neither presents sufficient justification for requiring Black women to tolerate such misogyny. The message that these arguments embrace—that patriarchy can be made to serve antiracist ends—is a familiar one, with proponents ranging from Eldridge Cleaver in the 1960s to Shahrazad Ali in the 1990s. In Gates's variant, the position of Black women is determined by the need to wield gargantuan penises in efforts to ridicule racist images of Black male sexuality. Even though Black women may not be the intended targets, they are necessarily called to serve these gargantuan penises and are thus in the position of absorbing the impact. The common message of all such strategies is that Black women are expected to be vehicles for notions of "liberation" that function to preserve Black female subordination.

To be sure, Gates's claim about the cultural aspects of 2 Live Crew's lyrics do address the legal issue about the applicability of the obscenity standard. As I indicated earlier, the group's music does have artistic and potentially political value; I believe the court decided this issue incorrectly and Will was all too glib in his critique. But these criticisms do not settle the issue within the community. Dozens and other wordplays have long been within the Black oral tradition, but acknowledging this fact does not eliminate the need to interrogate either the sexism within that tradition or the objectives to which that tradition has been pressed. To say that playing the dozens, for example, is rooted in a Black cultural tradition or that themes represented by mythic folk heroes such as Stagolee are Black does not settle the question of whether such practices are oppressive to women and others within the community. The same point can be made about the relentless homophobia in the work of Eddie Murphy and many other comedians and rappers. Whether or not the Black community has a pronounced tradition of homophobic humor is beside the point; the question instead is how these subordinating aspects of tradition play out in the lives of people in the community, people who are otherwise called upon to share the benefits and the burdens of a common history, culture, and political agenda. Although it may be true that the Black community is more familiar with the cultural forms that have evolved into rap, that familiarity should not end the discussion of whether the misogyny within rap is acceptable.

Moreover, we need to consider the possible relationships between sexism in our cultural practices and violence against women. Violence against women of color is not centered as a critical issue in either the antiracist or antiviolence discourses. The "different culture" defense may contribute to a disregard for women of color victimized by rape and violence that reinforces the tendency within the broader community not to take intraracial violence seriously. Numerous studies have suggested that Black victims of crime can count on less protection from the criminal justice system than whites receive. This is true for Black rape victims as well—their rapists are less likely to be convicted and on average serve less time when they are convicted. Could it be that perpetuating the belief that Blacks are different with respect to sexuality and violence contributes to the disregard of Black female rape victims like Bessie in *Native Son* or the woman thrown down an air shaft in Brooklyn?

Although there are times when Black feminists should fight for the integrity of Black culture, this does not mean that criticism must end when a practice or form of expression is traced to an aspect of culture. We must also determine whether the practices and forms of expression are consistent with other interests that we must define. The legal question of obscenity may be settled by finding roots in the culture. But traditional obscenity is not our central issue. Performances and representations that do not appeal principally to "prurient interests" or that may reflect expressive patterns that are culturally specific may still encourage self-hatred, disrespect, subordination, and various other manifestations of intragroup pathology. These problems require an internal group dialogue. Although we have no plenary authority to grapple with these issues, we do need to find ways of using group formation mechanisms and other social spaces to reflect upon and reformulate our cultural and political practices.

I said earlier that the political goals of Black feminism are to construct and empower a political sensibility that opposes misogyny and racism simultaneously. Merging this double vision in an analysis of the 2 Live Crew controversy makes clear that despite the superficial defense of the prosecution as being in the interests of women, nothing about the anti–2 Live Crew movement is about

Black women's lives. The political process involved in legal prosecution of 2 Live Crew's representational subordination of Black women does not seek to empower Black women; indeed, the racism of that process is injurious to us.

The implication of this conclusion is not that Black feminists should stand in solidarity with the supporters of 2 Live Crew. The spirited defense of 2 Live Crew was no more about defending the Black community than the prosecution was about defending women. After all, Black women—whose assault is the very subject of the representation—are part of that community. Black women can hardly regard the right to be represented as rape-deserving bitches and whores as essential to their interests. Instead the defense primarily functions to protect the cultural and political prerogative of male rappers to be as misogynistic as they want to be.

The debate over 2 Live Crew illustrates how the discursive structures of race and gender politics continue to marginalize Black women, rendering us virtually voiceless. Fitted with a Black feminist sensibility, one uncovers other issues in which the unique situation of Black women renders a different formulation of the problem than the version that dominates in current debate. Ready examples include rape, domestic violence, and welfare dependency. A Black feminist sensibility might also provide a more direct link between the women's movement and traditional civil rights movements, helping them both to shed conceptual blinders that limit the efficacy of their efforts. In the recent controversy over the nomination of Clarence Thomas to the U.S. Supreme Court, for example, organized groups in both camps—in particular women's groups—initially struggled to produce evidence showing Thomas's negative disposition toward their respective constituencies. Thomas's repeated derogatory references to his sister as the quintessential example of welfare dependency might have been profitably viewed from a Black feminist framework as the embodiment of his views on race, gender, and class, permitting an earlier formulation of a more effective coalition.

The development of a Black feminist sensibility is no guarantee that Black women's interests will be taken seriously. For that sensibility to develop into empowerment, Black women will have to make it clear that patriarchy is a critical issue that negatively impacts the lives of not only African-American women, but men as well. Within the African-American political community, this recognition might reshape traditional practices so that evidence of racism would not constitute sufficient justification for uncritical rallying around misogynistic politics and patriarchal values. Although collective opposition to racist practice has been and continues to be crucially important in protecting Black interests, an empowered Black feminist sensibility would require that the terms of unity no longer reflect priorities premised upon the continued marginalization of Black women.

6

Epilogue:
Burning Crosses and the R. A. V. Case

Mari J. Matsuda and Charles R. Lawrence III

In the early morning hours of June 21, 1990, long after they had put their five children to bed, Russ and Laura Jones were awakened by voices outside their house. Russ got up, went to his bedroom window, and peered into the dark. "I saw a glow," he recalled. There, in the middle of his yard, was a burning cross.[1] The Joneses are African Americans. In the spring of 1990 they had moved into their four-bedroom, three-bathroom dream house in St. Paul, Minnesota. They were the only Black family on the block. Two weeks after they had settled into their predominantly white neighborhood, the tires on both of their cars were slashed. A few weeks later one of their car windows was shattered, and a group of teenagers walked past their house and shouted "nigger" at their nine-year-old son. And now this burning cross. Russ Jones did not have to guess at the meaning of this symbol of racial hatred. There is no Black person in America who has not learned the significance of this instrument of persecution and intimidation, who has not had emblazoned on his or her mind the image of Black men's scorched bodies hanging from trees.

The assailant who burned the makeshift cross in the fenced yard of the Jones home was identified and prosecuted under a local hate crime ordinance. Following the predictable pattern identified in the introduction to this book, the defendant claimed the assaultive act was protected by the first amendment: Burning a cross is political speech, and any ordinance directed against such speech is thus unconstitutional. The Minnesota Supreme Court rejected this argument. Citing Mari Matsuda's work, the court found:

Burning a cross in the yard of an African American family's home is deplorable conduct that the City of St. Paul may without question prohibit. The burning cross is itself an unmistakable symbol of violence and hatred based on virulent notions of racial supremacy. It is the responsibility, even the obligation, of diverse communities to confront such notions in whatever form they appear.[2]

The Minnesota judges thus adopted a perspective urged by critical race theorists. They looked to history and context to understand the effect of a cross burning. Unlike ordinary trespassing or littering on someone's front lawn, the burning cross is inextricably tied to violence, to lynching, and to exclusion. Crosses burn to warn newcomers out of segregated neighborhoods, to silence whites who speak up in favor of racial tolerance, to draw upon and promote the fear that began with the nightriders of the Reconstruction era and continues to this day in the rituals of skinheads, Klansmen, and local thugs. Attackers use this symbol precisely because of the extreme and concrete distress it causes. Their aim is to cause harm, to silence and to exclude. As with death threats and fraud, the goal of cross burning is accomplished through speech. As we have argued throughout this book, however, ending the analysis at the determination that hate speech *is* speech is simplistic and doctrinally unworkable. It is also an affirmative harm to those whose injury goes unredressed by law.

In a climate of media attention focused on right-wing claims that a powerful "politically correct movement" was overrunning the nation, disempowering and silencing conservative white men, the Supreme Court of the United States agreed in June 1991 to review the Minnesota cross-burning case. Critical race theorists were immediately concerned that the Reagan-Bush Court took on the case in order to further dismantle civil rights gains. We were thus not surprised at Justice Antonin Scalia's opinion declaring the anti–cross-burning ordinance unconstitutional. Local governments, Scalia held, may prohibit littering or arson on peoples' lawns, but they may not single out racially motivated acts, such as cross burning, for criminalization. The decision thus limits the ability to treat the racist assault of cross burning as a particularly serious crime.

Justice Scalia's opinion in the *R.A.V.* case, as the cross-burning case is now known, was a clear example of exactly the kind of legal analysis this book is intended to counter.[3] It is completely ahistorical and acontextual. The Jones family's terror at finding a cross burning in their yard in the middle of the night is nowhere described. We are told that a "crudely made cross" was burned in the yard of a Black family, but we are told nothing about that family or the hostility they experienced upon moving into the neighborhood. The Ku Klux Klan, lynching, nightriders, the Reconstruction, continuing patterns of hate crimes and racial violence in this country are never mentioned. Hate crime statistics and social science evidence showing increasing use of burning crosses and swastikas to harass ethnic and religious minorities are not mentioned. The many reported cases in which state and federal courts have struggled to protect schoolchildren, voters, homeowners, workers, and other citizens from ethnic intimidation by cross burners are neither discussed nor cited. In effect, the opinion proceeds as though we know nothing about the origins of the practice of cross burning or about the meaning that a burning cross carries both for those who use it and those whom it terrorizes.

What we do learn from the opinion is that cross burning is not a "majority preference" and that the ordinance reflects inappropriate "special hostility" against "particular biases."[4] The cross burners are portrayed as an unpopular minority that the Supreme Court must defend against the power of the state. The injury to the Jones family is appropriated and the cross burner is cast as the injured victim. The reality of ongoing racism and exclusion is erased and bigotry is redefined as majoritarian condemnation of racist views. The powerful impact of the burning cross—the assault, the terror—is also inverted. The power is replaced in the hands of those who oppose racism. The powerful antiracists have captured the state and will use the state to oppress powerless racists. As a final element to this upside-down story, the Reagan-Bush judges are cast as the defenders of the down-trodden, the courageous upholders of the bill of rights.

This inverted story will no doubt surprise the many local lawmakers and law-enforcement officials who are struggling daily to keep the lid on the pressure cooker of racial animosity. Hate crime ordinances came about not because local legislators were bent on oppressing a tiny minority of unpopular racists, but because hate crimes had reached such an epidemic proportion that no one concerned with keeping the peace could ignore them. Civil rights organizations struggled mightily to raise public consciousness about the prevalence of hate crimes and to show how the targets of hate crimes were disempowered, silenced, and disenfranchised. None of this is mentioned in the Scalia opinion, however. Instead, local legislators dealing responsibly with local problems are painted as group-think imposers of orthodoxy.

Concurring Justices Byron White, Harry Blackmun, Sandra Day O'Connor, and John Paul Stevens would also overturn the St. Paul ordinance for overbreadth, but they would not prohibit all local efforts to prevent cross burnings and other forms of bigoted intimidation. Two of these Justices condemn the Scalia opinion for turning first amendment doctrine "on its head." While the critique is intended as a doctrinal one, for the Scalia opinion both misstates and revises existing doctrine in confusing and astonishing ways, it also echoes the political critique made by critical race theorists. Judges from Oliver Wendell Holmes to Harry Blackmun have not had to be radicals to recognize the simple truth that doing justice requires more than manipulating doctrine in a vacuum. The concurring opinions explicitly discuss the harm of cross burnings and respect the determination of local lawmakers that the threat to society from burning crosses is greater than the threat from burning trash.

Where does the *R.A.V.* decision leave us? It provides little guidance for legislators, school administrators, and community activists who are attempting to deal with the racism that—Supreme Court erasures notwithstanding—still plagues our neighborhoods and institutions. The *R.A.V.* decision will not outlive the problem of racism, and, indeed, its incoherence and illogic are unlikely to withstand the test of even a few year's time. We urge those concerned about racism to continue their creative efforts to respond to assaultive speech, guided by the reality of racism's concrete harms. This requires listening carefully to the stories of families who spend the night imprisoned by fear while crosses burn and linking that to the broad gulfs that separate, still, the life chances of haves and have-nots in America. As critical race theorists, we do not separate cross burning from police brutality nor epithets from infant mortality rates. We believe there are systems of culture, of privilege, and of power that intertwine in complex ways to tell a sad and continuing story of insider/outsider. We choose to see and to struggle against a world made by burning crosses.

In this book we have argued for an antisubordination interpretation of the first amendment. The first amendment goal of maximizing public discourse is not attained in a marketplace of ideas distorted by coercion and privilege. Burning crosses do not bring to the table more ideas for discussion, and the Court's failure to see this is part of a long history of not seeing what folks on the bottom see. We hold faith that a critical view of law can reconstruct the first amendment to bring the voices of the least to the places of power. In arguing against existing law, we argue not against law but for a legal world worthy of democracy's name.

Notes

Chapter 1

1. *See* H. Ehrlich, Campus Ethnoviolence and the Policy Options (National Institute Against Prejudice & Violence, Institute Report No. 4, Mar. 5, 1990).

2. V. Harding, There Is a River (1981).

3. Hayward & Marsh, *Two Racial Incidents Strike Ujamaa House,* Stanford Daily, Oct. 17, 1988, at 1.

4. P. Freire, Pedagogy of the Oppressed 75 (1982).

5. Matsuda, Address to the American Assoc. of Law Schools, Constitutional Law Section, Washington, DC (Jan. 5, 1991).

Chapter 2

1. Incidents such as this are described in P. Sims, The Klan 167–72 (1978).

2. At the University of California Hastings College of the Law, someone defaced a Black History Month Display in just such a manner. *Racist Caricatures Anger Students,* Recorder (San Francisco), Feb. 11, 1989, at 1.

3. Author's personal experience, Perth, Western Australia, July 1987, recounted in *Language as Violence v. Freedom of Expression: Canadian and American Perspectives on Group Defamation,* 37 Buffalo L. Rev. 337 (1989) (transcript of the James McCormick Mitchell Lecture, State University of New York at Buffalo School of Law, Nov. 4, 1988) [hereinafter cited as *Language as Violence*].

4. L. Bollinger, The Tolerant Society: Free Speech and Extremist Speech in America (1986).

5. Collin v. Smith, 447 F. Supp. 676 (N.D. Ill.) *affd.,* 578 F.2d 1197 (7th Cir.) *cert. denied,* 439 U.S. 916 (1978); Village of Skokie v. National Socialist Party, 51 Ill. App. 3d 279, 366 N.E.2d 347 (1977), *modified,* 69 Ill. 2d 605, 373 N.E.2d 21 (1978).

6. Monture, *Ka-Nin-Geh-Heh-Gah-E-Sa-Nonh-Yah-Gah,* 2 Canadian Journal of Women's Law 159 (1986).

7. D. Bell, And We Are Not Saved (1987).

8. Williams, *Spirit-Murdering the Messenger: The Discourse of Fingerpointing as the Law's Response to Racism,* 42 Miami L. Rev. 127, 139 (1987).

9. *See* Critchen v. Firestone Steel Prods. Co. Nos. 12,190–EM & 15,389–EM (Mich. Civ. Rts. Comm'n May 23, 1984) *reported in* 1984 Michigan Civ. Rts. Commission, Case Digest 13, 17–18.

10. *S.F. Fire Department Declared "Out of Control,"* Asian L. Caucus Rep., July–Dec. 1987, at 1, col. 1.

11. Poverty Law Report, Mar.–Apr. 1982, at 11, col. 2.

12. *Black F.B.I. Agent's Ordeal: Meanness That Never Let Up,* N.Y. Times, Jan. 25, 1988, at 1, col. 1.

13. Complaint at 3, EEOC v. Hyster Co., Civ. No. 88-930-DA (D. Ore., filed Aug. 15, 1988) (alleging a hostile work environment created by racially objectionable advertisement campaign and use of racial slurs by management in work place). An answer denying those allegations was filed by the defendant.

14. *Racial Violence Belies Good Life in Contra Costa County,* L.A. Times, Dec. 7, 1980, at 3, col. 5.

15. Asian and Pacific Islander Advisory Comm., Office of Attorney Gen. Cal. Dept. of Justice, Final Report 45 (1988).

16. Ga. State Advisory Comm'n to the U.S. Comm'n on Civil Rights, Perceptions of Hate Group Activity in Georgia 3 (1983) (testimony of Stuart Lowengrub, Southeastern Regional Director, Anti-Defamation League of B'nai B'rith, Atlanta).

17. *Cf.* Cover, *Violence and the Word,* 95 Yale L.J. 1601 (1986) (noting that the process of interpretation of legal language is ultimately bound to the imposition of violence).

18. Cervantes, *Poem for the Young White Man Who Asked Me How I, An Intelligent Well Read Person Could Believe in the War Between Races,* Emplumada (1981).

19. Williams, *supra* note 8, at 129.

20. Greenberg & Pyszcynski, *The Effect of an Overheard Ethnic Slur on Evaluation of the Target: How to Spread a Social Disease,* 21 J. Experimental Soc. Psychology 61, 70 (1985).

21. G. Allport, The Nature of Prejudice 461–78 (1954); H. Kitano, Race Relations 113–14 (1974); H. Schuman, C. Steeh & L. Bobo, Racial Attitudes in America 137 (1985).

22. *See, e.g.,* Afro-American Writing (R. Long & E. Collier eds. 1985).

23. International Convention on the Elimination of All Forms of Racial Discrimination *opened for signature* Mar. 7, 1966, 660 U.N.T.S. 195 [hereinafter Racial Discrimination Convention].

24. *See* N. Lerner, The U.N. Convention on the Elimination of All Forms of Racial Discrimination 43–53 (2d ed. 1980).

25. Revised draft of article 4 submitted to the Sub-Commission by Mr. Abram, Sub-Commission on Prevention of Discrimination and Protection of Minorities, U.N. Doc. E/CN4/Sub. 2/L. 308/Add. 1/Rev. 1 (1964). This view is consistent with U.S. case law. *See, e.g.,* Brandenburg v. Ohio, 395 U.S. 444 (1969).

26. Draft of article 4 submitted by Messrs. Ivanov and Ketrzynski, Sub-Commission on Prevention of Discrimination and Protection of Minorities, U.N. Doc. E/CN 4/ Sub. 2/ L. 314 (1964).

27. See N. Lerner, *supra* note 24, at 44–45.

28. *Id.* at 46.

29. *Id.*

30. *See id.* at 71–73.

31. Racial Discrimination Convention, *supra* note 23, at 218.

32. *Id.* at 214.

33. 20 U.N. Gaor (1406th plen. mtg.) 7, U.N. Doc. A/PV. 1406 (1965).

34. Vienna Convention on the Law of Treaties, May 23, 1969, art. 18, 1155 U.N.T.S. 331, 336.

35. N. Nathanson & E. Schwelb, The United States and the United Nations Treaty on Racial Discrimination 8 (Studies in Transnational Legal Policy No. 9, 1975).

36. *Id.* at 85.

37. Council of Europe, European Convention on Human Rights: Collected Texts §1 (7th ed. 1971).

38. Pan American Union, Final Act of the Ninth International Conference of American States 38 (1948).

39. The Convention on the Prevention and Punishment of the Crime of Genocide, art. 3(c), *adopted* Dec. 9, 1948, 78 U.N.T.S. 277, 280, requires member states to prohibit "[d]irect and public incitement to commit genocide." The convention was ratified by the U.S. Senate in 1986 with reservations noting that the U.S. Constitution would override any provisions of the convention, 132 Cong. Rec. 2349-50 (Feb. 19, 1986).

40. Race Relatons Act, 1965, c. 73 §6(1), amended in 1976 and 1986.

41. *See* Race Relations Act, of 1976, c. 74 §70.

42. I. MacDonald, Race Relations and Immigration Law ¶8 (1969).

43. Can. Rev. Stat. ch. C-46 §§318, 319 (1985).

44. Constitution Act of 1982, §2.

45. *See, e.g.,* the proposed amendments to the New South Wales Racial Discrimination Act reported in Woomera, June/July 1987, at 1 (allowing group defamation actions for racial slurs). Violent racist groups are gaining in membership and visibility in Australia.

46. Gertz v. Robert Welch, Inc., 418 U.S. 323, 339 (1974).

47. Knights of the Ku Klux Klan v. East Baton Rouge Parish School Bd., 679 F.2d 64 (5th Cir. 1982) (school board thwarted in effort to stop KKK meeting in gym, but no fees awarded to KKK); Coen v. Harrison County School Bd., 638 F.2d 24 (5th Cir. 1981) (KKK granted permission to use public ball park; no fees against city); Collin v. Chicago Park Dist., 460 F.2d 746 (7th Cir. 1972) (first amendment right of access for Nazis to speak in public park).

48. *See* Collin v. Smith, 578 F.2d at 1209 ("the governmental interest . . . could more narrowly be served by . . . marshalling local, county, and state police to prevent violations").

49. Schauer, *Categories and the First Amendment: A Play in Three Acts,* 34 Vand. L. Rev. 265, 270 (1981).

50. Collin v. Smith, 447 F. Supp. 676 (N.D. Ill.) *affd.* 578 F.2d 1197 (7th Cir.), *cert. denied,* 439 U.S. 916 (1978); Village of Skokie v. National Socialist Party, 51 Ill. App. 3d 279, 366 N.E. 2d 347 (1977), *modified,* 69 Ill. 2d 605, 373 N.E. 2d 21 (1978).

51. Regents of the Univ. v. Bakke, 438 U.S. 265, 407 (1978) (Blackmun, J., dissenting).

52. Delgado, *Derrick Bell and the Ideology of Racial Reform,* 97 Yale L. J. 923, 937 (1988).

53. *See A Theory Goes on Trial,* Time, Sept. 24, 1984, at 62 (Dr. Shockley, who admits to subscribing to the white supremacist publication *Thunderbolt,* is called "nearly incompetent" by trained geneticist).

54. Address by Elie Wiesel, Hofstra University Conference on Group Defamation and Freedom of Speech (Apr. 20, 1988).

55. From a clip-out coupon in a two-page advertisement for a Time-Life book series, Sports Illustrated, Feb. 6, 1989, at 42–43. The ad included portraits of S.S. figures and a small, color-highlighted swastika in the lower left-hand corner. It in no way suggested approval of S.S. activities, although it did make me uneasy in its tone of fascination.

56. Statement of a judge handling a farm worker's case, reported in *Judge Bradshaw: Bad Humor Man,* Food and Justice, Apr. 1988, at 8 (a publication of the United Farm Workers).

57. *Do the Right Thing* (Universal Pictures 1989).

58. *Black Students Forgive Teacher's Mistaken Slur,* N.Y. Times, Oct. 17, 1988, col. 1.

59. I thank my colleague Dr. Chalsa Loo, a psychologist, college counselor, and specialist in multicultural interaction, for these insights.

60. *See* Delgado, *Minority Law Professors' Lives: The Bell-Delgado Survey,* 24 Harv. Civ. Rts.–Civ. Lib. L. Rev. 407 (1989) (reporting on widespread effects of discrimination and high attrition rates among minority law teachers); Chused, *The Hiring and Retention of Minorities and Women on American Law School Faculties,* 137 U. Pa. L. Rev. 537 (1988); Haines, *Minority Law Professors and the Myth of Sisyphus: Consciousness and Praxis Within the Special Teaching Challenges in American Law Schools,* 10 Nat'l Black L.J. 247 (1988); McGee, *Symbol and Substance in the Minority Professoriat's Future,* 3 Harv. BlackLetter J. 67 (1986) (special burdens and obligations of minority law professors).

61. Kunz v. New York, 340 U.S. 290, 299 (1951) (Jackson, J., dissenting).

62. B. Christian, "Somebody Forgot to Tell Somebody Something": African-American Women's Historical Novels 21 (Paper delivered at the University of Hawaii Apr. 1989) (on file with author).

63. *See* Johnson, *Can the State Unmask the Klan?* Ky. Bench & Bar, Apr. 1981, at 8 (citing statutes in California, Michigan, Kentucky, North Carolina, Alabama, Florida, South Carolina, Tennessee, Virginia, Oklahoma, and Louisiana. Some statutes contain useful exemptions for Halloween, Mardi Gras, and Gasparilla).

64. Annotation, *Libel and Slander: Imputation of Association with Persons of Race or Nationality as to Which There Is Social Prejudice,* 121 A.L.R. 1151, 1151 (1939) (citing Sharp v. Bussey, 137 Fla. 96, 187 So. 779 [1939]).

65. MacKinnon, *Not a Moral Issue,* 2 Yale L. & Pol'y. Rev. 321 (1984).

66. Ga. State Advisory Comm'n to the U.S. Comm'n on Civil Rights, *supra* note 16, at 21.

67. Llewellyn, *Some Realism About Realism—Responding to Dean Pound,* 44 Harv. L. Rev. 1222, 1236 (1931) ("The conception of law as a means to social ends and not an end in itself").

Chapter 3

1. W.E.B. DuBois, The Souls of Black Folk 16–17 (1953).

2. V. Harding, There Is a River 82 (1981).

3. 347 U.S. 483 (1954).

4. Karst, *Citizenship, Race and Marginality,* 30 Wm. & Mary L. Rev. 1, 1 (1988).

5. 347 U.S. at 494.

6. 163 U.S. 537 (1896).

7. *Id.* at 560 (J. Harlan, dissenting).

8. *See, e.g.,* Strossen, *Regulating Racist Speech on Campus: A Modest Proposal?* Duke L. J. 484 at 541–43 (1990).

9. L. Tribe, American Constitutional Law §12–7 at 827 (2d ed. 1988).

10. 42 U.S.C. §2000a (1982).

11. K. Thomas, Comments at Frontiers of Legal Thought Conference, Duke Law School (Jan. 26, 1990).

12. C. MacKinnon, Toward a Feminist Theory of the State 204 (1989).

13. Jones v. Alfred H. Mayer Co., 392 U.S. 409, 439 (1968) (upholding Congress's use of the "badge of servitude" idea to justify federal legislation prohibiting racially discriminatory practices by private persons).

14. Michelman, *Conceptions of Democracy in American Constitutional Argument: The Case of Pornography Regulation,* 56 Tenn. L. Rev. 291, 306 (1989).

15. 109 U.S. 3 (1883).

16. 410 U.S. 113 (1973).

17. 448 U.S. 297, 316 (1980).

18. *See* Michelman, *supra* note 14, at 306–07.

19. U.S. Const. art. I, §2, cl. 3 and §9, cl. 1; art. IV, §2, cl. 3.

20. Dred Scott v. Sanford, 60 U.S. (19 How.) 393 (1857).

21. 339 U.S. 637 (1950).

22. *A Step Toward Civility,* Time, May 1, 1989, at 43.

23. *Id.*

24. Heart of Atlanta Motel, Inc. v. United States, 379 U.S. 241, 258 (1964); *see also* Roberts v. United States Jaycees, 468 U.S. 609, 624 (1984) (Court upheld the public accommodations provision of the Minnesota Human Rights Act).

25. 461 U.S. 574, 595 (1983).

26. 461 U.S. at 604.

27. Interpretation of the Fundamental Standard defining when verbal or nonverbal abuse violates the student conduct code adopted by the Stanford University Student Conduct Legislative Council, March 14, 1990. *SCLC Offers Revised Reading of Standard,* Stanford Daily, Apr. 4, 1990, §1, col. 4.

It is important to recognize that this regulation is not content neutral. It prohibits "discriminatory harassment" rather than just plain harassment, and it regulates only discriminatory harassment based on "sex, race, color, handicap, religion, sexual orientation, and national and ethnic origin." It is arguably viewpoint neutral with respect to these categories, although its reference to "words . . . that, by virtue of their form, are commonly understood to convey direct and visceral hatred or contempt" probably means that there will be many more epithets that refer to subordinated groups than words that refer to superordinate groups covered by the regulation.

28. Chaplinsky v. New Hampshire, 315 U.S. 568, 572 (1942).

29. *See* Cohen v. California, 403 U.S. 15, 21 (1971) (holding that the state could not excise, as offensive conduct, particular epithets from public discourse); Erznoznik v. City of Jacksonville, 433 U.S. 205, 209 (1975) (overturning a city ordinance that deterred drive-in theaters from showing movies containing nudity).

30. *See* Kovacks v. Cooper, 336 U.S. 77, 86 (1949) (right to free speech not abridged by city ordinance outlawing use of sound trucks on city streets); Federal Communications Comm'n v. Pacifica Found., 438 U.S. 726, 748 (1978) (limited first amendment protection of broadcasting that extends into privacy of home); Rowan v. United States Post Office Dep't, 397 U.S. 728, 736 (1970) (unwilling recipient of sexually arousing material had right to instruct Postmaster General to cease mailings to protect recipient from unwanted communication of "ideas").

31. Letter from Dulany O. Bennett to parents, alumni, and friends of the Wilmington Friends School (May 17, 1988).

32. 347 U.S. at 494.

33. L. Tribe, *supra* note 9, at 861.

34. 376 U.S. 254, 270.

35. 418 U.S. 323, 339 (1974).

36. 343 U.S. 250 (1952).

37. J. Ely, Democracy and Distrust, 103–04, 135–79 (1980).

38. J.S. Mill, On Liberty, ch. 2 (1859).

39. J. Madison, The Federalist No. 51, at 323–24 (C. Rossiter ed. 1961).

40. MacKinnon, *Not a Moral Issue,* 2 Yale L. & Pol'y Rev. 321, 325–26, 335 (1984).

41. C. MacKinnon, *supra* note 12, at 206.

42. D. Bell, Racism and American Law, 30 (2nd ed. 1980).

43. R. Delgado, Address to State Historical Society, Madison, Wis. (Apr. 24, 1989). Delgado drew an analogy to Susan Brownmiller's observation that rape is the crime of all men against all women. Men who would never commit rape and who abhor it nonetheless benefit from the climate of terror that the experience of rape helps create.

44. 721 F.Supp. 852 (1989).

Chapter 4

1. 88 Wash.2d 735, 565 P.2d 1173 (1977) (en banc).

2. 578 F.2d 1197 (7th Cir.), *cert. denied,* 439 U.S. 916 (1978).

3. P. Mason, Race Relations 2 (1970).

4. O. Cox, Caste, Class and Race 383 (1948).

5. K. Clark, Dark Ghetto 63–64 (1965).

6. J. Kovel, White Racism: A Psychohistory 195 (1970).

7. J. Martin & C. Franklin, Minority Group Relations 3 (1979).

8. Kiev, *Psychiatric Disorders in Minority Groups,* in Psychology and Race 416, 420–24 (P. Watson ed. 1973).

9. Harburg, Erfurt, Hauenstein, Chape, Schull & Schork, *Socio-Economical Stress, Suppressed Hostility, Skin Color, and Black-White Male Blood Pressure: Detroit,* 35 Psychosomatic Med. 276 (1973).

10. J. Martin & C. Franklin, *supra* note 7, at 43. *See* G. Allport, The Nature of Prejudice 138 (1958).

11. Allport, *The Bigot in Our Midst,* 40 Commonweal 582 (1944), *reprinted in* Anatomy of Racial Prejudice 161, 164 (G. deHuszar ed. 1946).

12. M. Goodman, Race Awareness in Young Children (rev. ed. 1964).

13. M. Deutsch, I. Katz & A. Jensen, Social Class, Race and Psychological Development 175 (1968).

14. M. Goodman, *supra* note 12, at 246.

15. K. Keniston, All Our Children 33 (1977).

16. G. Allport, *supra* note 10, at 139.

17. P. van den Berghe, Race and Racism 21 (2d ed. 1978).

18. *Id.* at 20.

19. *Id.* at 20.

20. G. Allport, The Nature of Prejudice 472 (1954).

21. R. Williams, The Reduction of Intergroup Tensions 73 (1947).

22. G. Allport, *supra* note 10, at 437.

23. *Id.*

24. *Id.* at 439.

25. H. Triandis, *The Impact of Social Change on Attitudes,* in Attitudes, Conflict and Social Changes 132 (1972) (quoted in Katz, *Preface* to Toward the Elimination of Racism 8 [P. Katz ed. 1976]).

26. G. Myrdal, An American Dilemma xliii (1944).

27. 424 S.W.2d 627 (Tex. 1967).

28. Restatement (Second) of Torts § 46 (1965). Some states have adopted the Restatement view.

29. Alcorn v. Anbro Eng'g, Inc., 2 Cal. 3d 493, 498, 468 P.2d 216, 218, 86 Cal. Rptr. 88, 90 (1970).

30. Samms v. Eccles, 11 Utah 2d 289, 293, 358 P.2d 344, 347 (1961).

31. Harned v. E-Z Fin. Co., 151 Tex. 641, 254 S.W.2d 81 (1953).

32. 2 Cal. 3d 493, 468 P.2d 216, 86 Cal. Rptr. 88 (1970).

33. 25 Cal. 3d 932, 603 P.2d 58, 160 Cal. Rptr. 141 (1979).

34. 355 F. Supp. 206 (S.D. Fla. 1973).

35. 100 So. 2d 396 (Fla. 1958).

36. 46 Ill. App. 3d 162, 360 N.E.2d 983 (1977).

37. I. Kan. 2d 213, 563 P.2d 511 (1977).

38. Restatement (Second) of Torts §46 comment d (1965).

39. Jones v. R.L. Polk & Co., 190 Ala. 243, 67 So. 577 (1915); Natchez Times Publishing Co. v. Dunigan, 221 Miss. 320, 72 So. 2d 681 (1954); Bowen v. Independent Publishing Co., 230 S.C. 590, 96 S.E.2d 564 (1957).

40. W. Keeton, D. Dobbs, R. Keeton & D. Owen, Prosser and Keeton on Torts, §111, at 771 (5th ed. 1984).

41. 42 U.S.C. § 1983 (1976 & Supp. III [1979]).

42. 605 F.2d 330 (7th Cir. 1976).

43. 284 F. Supp. 933 (E.D. Pa. 1968).

44. City of Minneapolis v. Richardson, 307 Minn. 80, 82–83, 239 N.W.2d 197, 200 (1976).

45. L.A. Times, Aug. 20, 1980, § I, at 1, col. 1.

46. No. 840149, King Co. (Wash.) Super. Ct. (July 31, 1978). *See* Seattle Times, Aug. 1, 1978, §A, at 1, col. 1.

47. Seattle Times, Aug. 1, 1978, § A, at 1, col. 1.

48. 52 N.Y.2d 72, 417 N.E.2d 525, 436 N.Y.S.2d 231 (1980).

49. 388 F. Supp. 603 (S.D. Ohio 1975).

50. 42 U.S.C. § 2000e-2(a)(2) (1976).

51. Ill. Const. art. I, § 20. The provision was derived from the criminal libel statute held constitutional in Beauharnais v. Illinois, 342 U.S. 250 (1952).

52. W. Prosser, Handbook of the Law of Torts, § 1, at 3–4 (4th ed. 1971).

53. *See* F. Michelman, *Property, Utility and Fairness: Comments on the Ethical Foundation of "Just Compensation" Law,* 80 Harv. L. Rev. 1165, 1192 (1967).

54. Masruder, *Mental and Emotional Disturbance in the Law of Torts,* 49 Harv. L. Rev. 1033, 1035 (1936).

55. W. Prosser, *supra* note 52, §52.

56. 2 Cal. 3d at 498 n.4, 468 P.2d at 219 n.4, 86 Cal. Rptr. at 91 n.4.

57. 88 Wash.2d at 742, 565 P.2d at 1177.

58. See W. Prosser, *supra* note 52, §54, at 327–28; McNiece, *Psychic Injury and Tort Liability in New York,* 24 St. John's L. Rev. 1, 31 (1949); Wade, *Tort Liability for Abusive and Insulting Language,* 4 Vand. L. Rev. 63, 77 (1950).

59. 315 U.S. 568 (1942).

60. 403 U.S. 15 (1971).

61. 72 Yale L. J. 877, 878–86 (1963).

62. Emerson, 72 Yale L. J. 877, at 882 (1963).

63. *See* A. Meiklejohn, Free Speech and Its Relation to Self-Government (1948); A. Meiklejohn, Political Freedom (1960).

64. 413 U.S. 49 (1973).

65. Emerson, *supra* note 62, at 883 (quoting the Declaration of Independence ¶2 [U.S. 1776]).

66. Emerson, *supra* note 62, at 884–85.

Chapter 5

1. 137 Cong. Rec. S597, S610 (1991) (S. 15, H.R. 1502).

2. S. Ali, The Blackman's Guide to the Blackwoman (1989).

3. Pub. L. 99-639 (Nov. 10, 1986), Pub. L. 100–525, § 7(a)–(c) (Oct. 24, 1988).

4. S. Ali, *supra* note 2, at 169.

5. H.R. 1502, S. 15 (102d Cong.).

6. Coraham, *Custer May Be Shot Down Again in Battle of Sexes over X-Rated Video Game,* People Magazine, Nov. 15, 1982.

7. Santoro, *How 2B Nasty: Rap Musicians 2 Live Crew Arrested,* The Nation, July 2, 1990, at 4.

8. Will, *America's Slide into the Sewer,* Newsweek, July 30, 1990, at 64.

9. Gates, *2 Live Crew Decoded,* N.Y. Times, June 19, 1990, at A23.

10. *2 Live Crew,* UPI (Oct. 19, 1990).

11. 413 U.S. 15, 24 (1973).

12. *2 Live Crew,* UPI (Oct. 19, 1990).

13. 739 F. Supp. 578, 589 (S.D. Fla. 1990).

14. Will, *supra* note 8.

15. R. Wright, Native Son (1966).

16. Will, *supra* note 8.

17. *An Album Is Judged Obscene; Rap: Slick, Violent, Nasty and, Maybe Helpful,* N.Y. Times, June 17, 1990, at 1.

Chapter 6

1. This description is taken from a news report. See Tamar Lewin, *Hate-Crime Law Is Focus of Case on Free Speech,* N. Y. Times, Dec. 1, 1991, sec. 1 at 1.

2. In the Matter of the Welfare of R.A.V., 464 N.W.2d 507 at 508 (Minn. 1991).

3. R.A.V. are the initials of the defendant, who was a minor at the time of the prosecution.

4. R.A.V. v. St. Paul, 120 L. Ed. 2d 305 at 326 (1992).

Bibliography

Allport, Gordon W. The Nature of Prejudice (1954).

Arkes. *Civility and the Restriction of Speech: Rediscovering the Defamation of Groups,* 1974 Supreme Court Review 281.

Ball, Milner. *The Legal Academy and Minority Scholars,* 103 Harvard Law Review 1855 (1990).

Banks, Taunya L. *Two Life Stories: Reflections of One Black Woman Law Professor,* 6 Berkeley Women's Law Journal 46 (1991).

Barnes, Robin D. *Race Consciousness: The Thematic Content of Racial Distinctiveness in Critical Race Scholarship,* 103 Harvard Law Review 1864 (1990).

Bartlett, Katharine T., and O'Barr, Jean. *The Chilly Climate on College Campuses,* 1990 Duke Law Journal 574 (1990).

Bell, Derrick. And We Are Not Saved: The Elusive Quest for Racial Justice (1987). Race, Racism and American Law (2nd ed. 1980).

Bogle, Donald. Toms, Coons, Mulattoes, Mammies, and Bucks: An Interpretive History of Blacks in American Films (1973).

Bollinger, Lee C. The Tolerant Society: Free Speech and Extremist Speech in America (1986).

Brownmiller, Susan. Against Our Will: Men, Women and Rape (1975).

Caldwell, Paulette. *A Hair Piece: Perspectives on the Intersection of Race and Gender,* 1991 Duke Law Journal 385 (1991).

Calmore, John O. *Exploring the Significance of Race and Class in Representing the Black Poor,* 61 Oregon Law Review 201 (1982). *Toward Archie Shepp and the Return of Fire Music: Voicing Critical Race Theory and Securing an Authentic Intellectual Life in a Multicultural World* 64 Southern California Law Review (1992).

Chused, Richard H. *The Hiring and Retention of Minorities and Women on American Law School Faculties,* 137 University of Pennsylvania Law Review 537 (1988).

Clark, Herbert. Psychology and Language: An Introduction to Psycholinguistics (1977).

Colker, Ruth. *Anti-Subordination Above All: Sex, Race, and Equal Protection,* 61 New York University Law Review 1003 (1986).

Collins, Patricia H. Black Feminist Thought: Knowledge, Consciousness and the Politics of Empowerment (1990).

Cook, Anthony E. *Beyond Critical Legal Studies,* 103 Harvard Law Review 985 (1990).

Crenshaw, Kimberlè Williams. *A Black Feminist Critique of Anti-Discrimination Law and Politics,* in The Politics of Law (D. Kairys ed. 1990). *Demarginalizing the Intersection of Race and Sex: A Black Feminist Critique of Antidiscrimination*

Doctrine, Feminist Theory and Antiracist Politics, University of Chicago Legal Forum 139 (1989). *Race, Reform, and Retrenchment: Transformation and Legitimation in Anti-discrimination Law,* 101 Harvard Law Review 1331 (1988).

Cover, Robert. *Violence and the Word,* 95 Yale Law Journal 1601 (1986).

Culp, Jerome McCristal, Jr. *Toward a Black Legal Scholarship: Race and Original Understandings,* 1991 Duke Law Journal 39 (1991).

Dalton, Harlon. *The Clouded Prism,* 22 Harvard Civil Rights–Civil Liberties Law Review 435 (1987).

Davis, Peggy C. *Law as Microaggression,* 98 Yale Law Journal 1559 (1989).

Delgado, Richard. *Campus Anti-Racism Rules: Constitutional Narratives in Collision,* 85 Northwestern University Law Review 343 (1991). *Critical Legal Studies and the Realities of Race—Does the Fundamental Contradiction Have a Corollary?* 23 Harvard Civil Rights–Civil Liberties Law Review 407 (1989). *Epithets and Name-Calling,* 17 Harvard Civil Rights–Civil Liberties Law Review 133 (1982). *The Ethereal Scholar: Does Critical Legal Studies Have What Minorities Want?* 22 Harvard Civil Rights–Civil Liberties Law Review 301 (1987). *The Imperial Scholar: Reflections on a Review of Civil Rights Literature,* 132 University of Pennsylvania Law Review 561 (1984). *Minority Law Professors' Lives: The Bell-Delgado Survey,* 24 Harvard Civil Rights–Civil Liberties Law Review 349 (1989).

Denis, Martin K. *Race Harassment Discrimination: A Problem That Won't Go Away,* 10 Employment Relations Law Journal 415 (1984).

Dowd-Hall, Jacquelyn. *"The Mind That Burns in Each Body": Women, Rape, and Racial Violence,* in The Powers of Desire (A. Snitow ed. 1983).

DuBois, W.E.B. The Souls of Black Folk (1953).

Dworkin, Andrea. *Against the Male Flood: Censorship, Pornography, and Equality,* 8 Harvard Women's Law Journal 1 (1985). Pornography: Men Possessing Women (1980).

Ehrlich, Howard. Campus Ethnoviolence and the Policy Options (National Institute Against Prejudice and Violence, Institute Report No. 4, 1990).

Emerson, Thomas Irwin. The System of Freedom of Expression (1970).

Espinoza, Leslie. *Masks and Other Disguises: Exposing Legal Academia,* 103 Harvard Law Review 1878 (1990).

Estrich, Susan. *Rape,* 95 Yale Law Journal 1087 (1986).

Freeman, Alan. *Antidiscrimination Law: A Critical Review,* in The Politics of Law 96 (D. Kairys ed. 1982). *Legitimizing Racial Discrimination Through Anti-Discrimination Law: A Critical Review of Supreme Court Doctrine,* 62 Minnesota Law Review 1049 (1978).

Gale, Mary Ellen. *Reimagining the First Amendment,* 65 St. John's Law Review 119 (1991).

Gotanda, Neil. *A Critique of "Our Constitution Is Colorblind,"* 44 Stanford Law Review 1 (1991).

Greene, Linda S. *Tokens, Role Models and Pedagogical Politics: Lamentations of an African-American Female Law Professor,* 6 Berkeley Women's Law Journal 81 (1991).

Grey, Thomas C. *Civil Rights vs. Civil Liberties: The Case of Discriminatory Verbal Harassment,* 8 Social Philosophy & Policy 81 (1991).

Griffin, John Howard. Black like Me (1960).

Grillo, Trina. *The Mediation Alternative,* 100 Yale Law Journal 1545 (1991).

Guinier, Lani. *No Two Seats: The Elusive Quest for Political Equality,* 77 Virginia Law Review 1413 (1991). *The Triumph of Tokenism: The Voting Rights Act and the Theory of Black Electoral Success,* 89 Michigan Law Review 1077 (1991).

Haines, Andrew W. *Minority Law Professors and the Myth of Sisyphus: Consciousness and Praxis Within the Special Teaching Challenges in American Law Schools,* 10 National Black Law Journal 247 (1988).

Hall, David. *The Constitution and Race: A Critical Perspective,* 5 New York Law School Journal of Human Rights 229 (1988).

Harris, Angela. *Race and Essentialism in Feminist Legal Theory,* 42 Stanford Law Review 581 (1990).

Heins, Marjorie. *Banning Words: A Comment on "Words That Wound,"* 18 Harvard Civil Rights–Civil Liberties Law Review 585 (1983).

Higginbotham, A. Leon. In the Matter of Color (1978).

Himes, Chester. If He Hollers Let Him Go (1945).

Hine, Darlene Clark. *Rape and the Inner Lives of Black Women in the Middle West: Preliminary Thoughts on the Culture of Dissemblance,* in Unequal Sisters: A Multi-Cultural Read in U.S. Women's History (C. Dubois & V. Ruiz eds. 1990).

hooks, bell. Ain't I a Woman: Black Women and Feminism (1981).

Jones, Charles. *An Argument for Federal Protection Against Racially Motivated Crimes: 18 U.S.C. sec. 241 and the Thirteenth Amendment,* 21 Harvard Civil Rights–Civil Liberties Law Review 689 (1986).

Karst, Kenneth. *Boundaries and Reason: Freedom of Expression and the Subordination of Groups,* 1990 University of Illinois Law Review 95 (1990).

Kennedy, Duncan. *A Cultural Pluralist Case for Affirmative Action in Legal Academia,* 1990 Duke Law Journal 705 (1990).

King, Deborah H. *Multiple Jeopardy, Multiple Consciousness: The Context of a Black Feminist Ideology,* 14 Signs 42 (1988).

Kovel, Joel. White Racism: A Psychohistory (1970).

Kretzmer, David. *Freedom of Speech and Racism,* 8 Cardozo Law Review 445 (1987).

Lawrence III, Charles R. *A Dream: On Discovering the Significance of Fear,* 10 Nova Law Review 627 (1986). The Bakke Case: The Politics of Inequality (with Joel Dreyfuss 1979). *The Id, the Ego and Equal Protection: Reckoning with Unconscious Racism,* 39 Stanford Law Review 317 (1987). *If He Hollers Let Him Go: When Racism Dresses in Speech's Clothing,* 1990 Duke Law Journal 431 (1990). *The Word and the River: Pedagogy as Scholarship as Struggle,* 65 Southern California Law Review 2231 (1992).

Littleton, Christine. *Equality and Feminist Legal Theory,* 48 University of Pittsburgh Law Review 1043 (1987). *Feminist Jurisprudence: The Difference Method Makes,* 41 Stanford Law Review 751 (1989).

López, Gerald P. *Training Future Lawyers to Work with the Politically and Socially Subordinated: Anti-Generic Legal Education,* 91 West Virginia Law Review 305 (1988).

Love, Jean C. *Discriminatory Speech and the Tort of Intentional Infliction of Emotional Distress,* 47 Washington & Lee Law Review 123 (1990).

MacKinnon, Catharine. Feminism Unmodified: Discourses on Life and Law (1987). Sexual Harassment of Working Women: A Case of Sex Discrimination (1979). Toward a Feminist Theory of the State (1989).

Matsuda, Mari J. *Affirmative Action and Legal Knowledge: Planting Seeds in Plowed-Up Ground,* 11 Harvard Women's Law Journal 12 (1988). *Language as Violence v. Freedom of Expression: Canadian and American Perspectives on Group Defamation,* 37 Buffalo Law Review 337 (1989). *Looking to the Bottom: Critical Legal Studies and Reparations,* 22 Harvard Civil Rights–Civil Liberties Law Review 401 (1987). *Public Response to Racist Speech,* 87 Michigan Law Review 2320 (1989). *Voices of America: Accent, Anti-Discrimination Law and A Jurisprudence for the Last Reconstruction,* 100 Yale Law Journal 1329 (1991). *When the First Quail Calls: Multiple Consciousness as Jurisprudential Method,* 11 Women's Rights Law Reporter 7 (1989).

Marshall, Thurgood. *The Constitution: A Living Document,* 30 Howard Law Journal 623 (1987).

McGee, Henry. *Symbol and Substance in the Minority Professoriat's Future,* 3 Harvard BlackLetter Journal 67 (1986).

Meiklejohn, Alexander. Free Speech and Its Relation to Self-Government (1948). Political Freedom (1960).

Michelman, Frank. *Conceptions of Democracy in American Constitutional Argument: The Case of Pornography Regulation,* 56 Tennessee Law Review 291 (1989).

Minow, Martha. *Neutrality, Equality and Tolerance,* 22 Change 17 (Jan/Feb 1990). *The Supreme Court, 1986 Term—Foreword: Justice Engendered,* 101 Harvard Law Review 101 (1987).

Monture, Patricia A. *Ka-Nin-Geh-Heh-Gah-E-Sa-Nonh-Yah-Gah,* 2 Canadian Journal of Women and the Law 159 (1986).

Neier, Aryeh. Defending My Enemy (1979).

Peller, Gary. *Race Consciousness,* 1990 Duke Law Journal 758 (1990).

Pettigrew, Thomas F. *New Patterns of Racism: The Different Worlds of 1984 and 1964,* 37 Rutgers Law Review 673 (1985).

Post, Robert C. *Racist Speech, Democracy, and the First Amendment,* 32 William and Mary Law Review 267 (1991).

Prosser, William L. *Intentional Infliction of Emotional Distress: A New Tort,* 37 Michigan Law Review 874 (1939).

Rabinowitz, Mark A. *Nazis in Skokie: Fighting Words or Heckler's Veto?* 28 De Paul Law Review 259 (1979).

Reisman, David. *Democracy and Defamation: Control of Group Libel,* 42 Columbia Law Review 727 (1942).

Rosaldo, Renato. Culture and Truth: The Remaking of Social Analysis (1989).

Scales-Trent, Judy. *Black Women and the Constitution: Finding Our Place, Asserting Our Rights,* 24 Harvard Civil Rights–Civil Liberties Law Review 9 (1989). *Commonalities: On Being Black and White, Different and the Same,* 2 Yale Journal of Law and Feminism 305 (1990).

Schauer, Frederick. *Categories and the First Amendment: A Play in Three Acts,* 34 Vanderbilt Law Review 265 (1981).

Schrecker, Ellen. No Ivory Tower: McCarthyism and the Universities (1986).

Schultz, Bud, and Schultz, Ruth. It Did Happen Here: Recollections of Political Repression in America (1989).

Schuman, Howard, Steeh, Charlotte, and Bobo, Lawrence. Racial Attitudes in America (1985).

Shapiro, Herbert. White Violence and Black Response: From Reconstruction to Montgomery (1988).

Southern Poverty Law Center. The Ku Klux Klan: A History of Racism and Violence (3d ed. 1988).

Spillars, Hortense. *A Small Drama of Words,* in Powers of Desire (A. Snitow ed. 1983).

Strossen, Nadine. *Regulating Racist Speech on Campus: A Modest Proposal?* 1990 Duke Law Journal 484 (1990).

Sunstein, Cass. *Pornography and the First Amendment,* 1968 Duke Law Journal 589 (1968).

Thomas, Kendall. *A House Divided Against Itself: A Comment on "Mastery, Slavery, and Emancipation,"* 10 Cardozo Law Review 1461 (1989). *"Rouge et Noir" Reread: A Popular Constitutional History of the Angelo Herndon Case,* 65 Southern California Law Review (1992).

Torres, Gerald. *Critical Race Theory: The Decline of the Universalist Ideal and the Hope of Plural Justice—Some Observations and Questions of an Emerging Phenomenon,* 75 Minnesota Law Review 993 (1991). *The Mashpee Indian Case,* 1990 Duke Law Journal 625.

Wade, John W. *Tort Liability for Abusive and Insulting Language,* 4 Vanderbilt Law Review 63 (1950).

Walker, Alice. The Color Purple (1982).

Walker, Lenore E. The Battered Woman (1979). The Battered Woman Syndrome (1984). Terrifying Love: Why Battered Women Kill and How Society Responds (1989).

Williams, Patricia J. The Alchemy of Race and Rights (1991).

Williams, Robert A. The American Indian in Western Legal Thought (1990). *Taking Rights Aggressively: The Perils and Promise of Critical Legal Studies for People of Color,* 5 Law and Inequality: A Journal of Theory and Practice 103 (1987).

Woodward, C. Vann. The Strange Career of Jim Crow (Galaxy ed. 1964).

About the Book and Authors

Words, like sticks and stones, can assault; they can injure; they can exclude. In this important book, four prominent legal scholars from the tradition of critical race theory draw on the experience of injury from racist hate speech to develop a first amendment interpretation that recognizes such injuries. In their critique of "first amendment orthodoxy," the authors argue that only a history of racism can explain why defamation, invasion of privacy, and fraud are exempt from free-speech guarantees while racist and sexist verbal assaults are not.

The rising tide of verbal violence on college campuses has increased the intensity of the "hate speech" debate. This book demonstrates how critical race theory can be brought to bear against both conservative and liberal ideology to motivate a responsible regulation of hate speech. The impact of feminist theory is also evident throughout. The authors have provided a rare and powerful example of the application of critical theory to a real-life social problem.

This timely and necessary book will be essential reading for those experiencing the conflicts of free-speech issues on campus—students, faculty, administrators, and legislators—as well as for scholars of jurisprudence. It will also be a valuable classroom tool for teachers in political science, sociology, law, education, ethnic studies, and women's studies.

Mari J. Matsuda is professor at the School of Law and at the Center for Asian American Studies, University of California–Los Angeles. **Charles R. Lawrence III** is professor of law at Stanford University. **Richard Delgado** is Charles Inglis Thomson Professor of Law at the University of Colorado. **Kimberlè Williams Crenshaw** is professor of law at the University of California–Los Angeles.

Index